Super-Aging

THE MORAL DANGERS OF SEEKING IMMORTALITY

MARK MOORSTEIN

iUniverse, Inc.
New York Bloomington

Super-Aging
The Moral Dangers of Seeking Immortality

iUniverse books may be ordered through booksellers or by contacting:

iUniverse
1663 Liberty Drive
Bloomington, IN 47403
www.iuniverse.com
1-800-Authors (1-800-288-4677)

Because of the dynamic nature of the Internet, any Web addresses or links contained in this book may have changed since publication and may no longer be valid. The views expressed in this work are solely those of the author and do not necessarily reflect the views of the publisher, and the publisher hereby disclaims any responsibility for them.

ISBN: 978-1-4502-2346-1 (sc)
ISBN: 978-1-4502-2347-8 (ebook)

Printed in the United States of America

iUniverse rev. date: 04/12/2010

Dedication

To my father and to Mozella

TABLE OF CONTENTS

Preface

If each of us could live for 300 years, would we? Should we?

Super-aging has ignited a revolution. With more people surviving longer than ever, and benefitting from biotechnology and collective enlightenment, we can expect a major shift in the balance of society. The extension of life beyond a natural period promises not only hope for those with unfinished work, but a source of scientific discovery and economic opportunity. In addition to its many positive effects, however, we can expect problems. Super-aging necessarily will burden the productive young and trigger radical changes in science, government, nature, religion, and morality.

When Sarah Palin raised the specter of death panels in 2009, she triggered a moral reaction to the rationing of life. The image of experts choosing life and death for others, or guarding the entrances and exits of existence, infuriated everyone. The statements by Palin seemed little more than typical political hyperbole in the aftermath of a contentious presidential election. Yet we dismissed the more serious issues lying below the surface in our desire to stamp out the Bush years. Obama promised change, a more intelligent approach to healthcare and an enlightened view of biotechnology. The era of Obama so far has let bioethical issues slip through the cracks.

Given the advances of medicine and biotechnology, we have to face the imminent risks embedded in super-longevity. Common thinking seems to set rationing of life and death into two extreme political-economic camps: socialist and capitalist. One holds that rationing ought to occur through central planning. The other holds that the market, with its subtlety, makes wise decisions based on supply and demand—and wealth. As Jay Rosenberg writes, "Anyone contemplating opting for immortality would ... be well advised ... to get an early start on a good program of diversified conservative investments."[1]

In a revolutionary environment, neither of these approaches alone does very much. No one trusts bureaucrats to decide who lives and dies. And no one believes that the markets can do everything. Imagine who would step to the front of the line for super-aging if only influence or wealth determined life and death. One critic of my essay has insisted that the market will sort things out, that only a few ever will confront the issue—those who can afford it. However, it's clear that both governments and markets are easily corrupted, especially in non-competitive situations. I suspect that an executive at Goldman Sachs, flush with cash, might become the first to buy a ticket to eternity—but what good would he do as a super-ager? Perhaps he might set up an eternal trust fund for his family and his genome—especially if the rule against perpetuities falls by the wayside. Rather than reward society's best, would we inadvertently create a dynasty for the inherently greedy? What would a Hitler or a Stalin do to the markets through government intervention in order to preserve their mad ideologies?

Selection is more subtle than mere rationing by government fiat or wealth: it contains not only a fungible, quantitative aspect, but a qualitative one as well. Decisions of life and death depend not only on an economy, but on biology, morals, religion and a thousand other factors. Despite what we read in our constitution, all lives aren't equal.

The moral debate over the selection of life and death probably began when man first realized that the bounty of the Garden of Eden might be a myth. Neither resources nor life extend forever, which meant that some could live only if others died. Survival of the fittest made many of the hard choices moot: those too weak to endure shortages of food, or who no longer could walk, or those whose eyesight limited their view of predators, died long before others could sentence them to death by neglect or by any affirmative action. Only when society created surpluses and began to care about strangers did the hard moral choices of long life truly become evident.

While it's fairly obvious that nature has devised ingenious ways to protect life up to a point (of reproduction), it's not so obvious why nature eventually gives up on older humans. As many have noted, it takes far less in resources to support a child than an elderly person. Why can't humans live for 300 years? Nature seems strong in its process of building up the body, but equally strong in tearing it down. When nature sides with growth (as in young life), society may simply need to assist in the process. When nature desires to destroy something (through decay), society must marshal substantial strength to overpower even passive disintegration.

Unfortunately, the elderly occupy the southern side of the life-cycle. It takes far more to support an elderly person than a child—and ever more for the super-elderly. David Brooks, in a column in the *New York Times*, writes that "we are living in an age of reverse-generativity. Far from serving the young, the old are now taking from them. First, they are taking money. According to Julia Isaacs of the Brookings Institution, the federal government now spends $7 on the elderly for each $1 it spends on children."[2] The elderly have increasing healthcare needs, not to mention a decline in productivity.

Nevertheless, science often gallops to the rescue, fighting the ravages of aging. Ting Zhang argues that in any event the elderly aren't completely defenseless—they have special assets that can overcome their natural disadvantages: knowledge. In a knowledge economy, he asserts, the elderly can do well to cover their own costs (of health insurance and social security)—provided that society allows them to form their own businesses.[3] Many, like Zhang, have argued that with a little direction, the elderly in fact can support themselves better than they do now and that society can reduce costs more efficiently. For example, one way to even out the disproportionate costs of healthcare and social security is by requiring the elderly to work longer, taxing their benefits, denying government payments to wealthy seniors, forcing them to stay in better shape, and regulating their personal bad habits, such as smoking.

Still, no matter how basic these approaches might be, people die. As Lucretius observed, "[A] certain end of life is ordained for human kind. We cannot avoid death; we must meet it face to face … Nor, in truth, by prolonging life do we take away one jot from the span of death, for there is no subtraction whereby we may be less long dead. Therefore you may live on as many generations as you will, yet everlasting death still waits for you."[4]

For as long as we do live, the question still turns on how to allocate life and death: whether to make "positivist," socialist, central-commanded, or man-made choices—or whether to take our hands off the wheel and let God, nature, or the market decide. Perhaps a compromise puts us all somewhere in the middle.

In 1987 Daniel Callahan confronted the issue head on in his book *Setting Limits*—arguing that "intergenerational equity" should limit healthcare to the elderly. Given the increasing numbers of elderly and the advances of technology, the demand for healthcare on our economy will become a bottomless pit. Callahan's detractors immediately pounced on him because age, as a standard for limiting healthcare, would be unjust. In an updated version of the book, he responds:

> *[A]ge is a relevant and conspicuous variable in health care costs, and the elderly are more costly as a group than people of younger ages. The fact that many elderly people remain healthy most of their final years—and that there is a heterogeneous pattern of health care usage—does not change the fact that the average per capita costs of the elderly are significantly higher than for younger people. Public policy must take account of,*

> *and work with, those averages. They are what count in devising*
> *programs, in projecting future costs, and in estimating different*
> *health care needs. Age matters. ... It matters when, as we can*
> *now see, meeting the health care costs of the elderly as a group*
> *begins to threaten the possibility of meeting the needs of other*
> *age groups. In the nature of the case, moreover, there are no*
> *fixed boundaries to the amount of money that can be spent*
> *combating the effects of biological aging and attempt to forestall*
> *death in old age. It is an unlimited frontier.*[5]

As in any good debate, counter-reactions to Callahan's point of view have become more refined. Some, like Gregory Stock, a biophysicist, insist that the value of a healthy human more than offsets the social costs in keeping one alive for generations. An aggressive advocate of genetic modification, Stock has argued that the same science that saves younger lives can—and should—save the lives of the elderly. But as Gina Maranto notes, "[T]he great collective enterprise Stock envisions will in all likelihood be limited only to the small percentage of people who can afford or gain access to these technologies. Then the issue becomes what these *Übermenschen* might do with the rest of us."[6]

Aubrey de Grey, a gerontologist, joins Stock in arguing that science, in the long run, will figure out a way to resolve social problems as they arise. De Grey, however, takes the anti-Callahan point of view to the extreme. He not only argues that technology may keep a human alive for hundreds of years, but that it's the right of individual humans to live that long.

Rights, of course, presume a priority. If I have a *natural* right to eat, I can exercise it whenever and wherever I can obtain food. If I possess a *governmental* right to eat—let's say I petition the government for a special ration card for caviar—I have a power that allows me to take caviar from others and even compel them to provide it for me. My ration card gives me a privilege that implies public obligation.

It's easy to see the problems with both natural and governmental rights: the former favors the talented, as well as the bullies of society. The latter favors the needy, as well as the deserving. Deserving something may presume a system based on fair standards, or it could rest on wholly subjective, and possibly corrupt standards. There may be shortage of caviar. Then what?

Francis Fukuyama in *Our Posthuman Future* also questions whether a right isn't just another way of burying one claim by another.[7] As a lawyer, it's a familiar concept: in American law there are fundamental rights, similar in many ways to natural rights, such as the right to due process, speech, or religion, that supersede less important rights, such as the right to drive a car. But there also exist legislated or case law rights that mediate conflicts. Where does the right to an extended life arise or fit in? De Grey believes super-aging springs up as a fundamental right. If so, from where does it spring? Certainly religious figures such as Pope Paul II don't accept the theory that an extended life is basic or natural. If super-aging (specifically using governmental support) isn't fundamental, can courts and legislatures impose it on the rest of us? Can courts order the government to reallocate resources to extend human life?

Interestingly, a moot court case posed whether a sentient robot had a fundamental due process right to exist (by forbidding its owner not to shut it off). The moot court, obviously perplexed by the question, ruled "unless and until there is a change in the consciousness of flesh and blood voting people, sufficient to cause our laws to embrace the concept of machines with human consciousness, the proponents cannot expect … vindication in the courtroom. A new paradigm is not going to come about without a national debate in which diversities and ideas are expressed and considered, including those who believe conscious, sentient machines extend and enhance human life, and those who feel that the whole concept is an abomination to the moral order."[8]

It's easy to pass sentence on a machine, but less so on a human. I watched a debate recorded at the Edmonton Aging Symposium in 2007 between Stock and Callahan, and moderated by de Grey. Stock began by conceding that no one disagreed that a long life "in decrepitude" was even worthy of discussion. However, science and research could improve the quality of life, and allow the elderly to remain productive and essentially pay their way during a very long retirement. Callahan argued that life has a natural termination and the costs to society far outweigh the benefits. Callahan also stressed the need to focus research into quality of life rather than its mere extension. De Grey interjected that the government should spend money to determine whether an extended life is worth the effort.

There, in a capsule, lies the entire moral debate: should society invest in super-aging? Depending on whether one is young or old (Callahan is approximately 80, Stock 60, de Grey 46), positivist or religious, individualist or groupie, the view becomes different. The framework in many ways determines the position.

If Stock and de Grey prevail in their arguments in favor of genetic alteration for super-aging, it seems obvious that many will pay a high price for the benefit of a very few. While we all would like to see Lincoln or Mother Theresa survive for a very long time, it's only because of their ability to "do good" for society that we even consider letting people like them jump to the head of the line to super-aging. Do the rest of us even stand a chance?

My colleagues in the practice of law have asked me why I wrote this essay. The simple answer is that I like debate and the dialectical process. As a baby boomer in good health (I ski, swim, hike, and bike), I probably have a few decades left. But as Heidegger said, we live toward our deaths. How I die is perhaps more important than when I die. As an experienced (i.e. mature) trial attorney, I've learned that the skill of a good brief lies less in the personal opinions of the writer than in his or her ability to arrange good arguments of some cogent form. When I wrote *Frameworks: Conflict in Balance*, a study of the way nature and man moderate tension, I found that thinkers from the ancient Greeks to present polemicists structured their views in a similar manner—even as they seemingly used different language and order. I enjoy language, especially different languages, and so it seemed to me that if I could translate the vocabulary of disparate writers into a common tongue, perhaps a new picture of conflict would emerge. Indeed it did.

I found, for example, that Thomas Kuhn, in *The Structure of Scientific Revolutions*, paved the way in explaining the dynamic architecture of evolving theories. I tried to go farther in explaining conflict: frameworks (another term for paradigms) not only evolve, shift, and revolt, but contain rules as well as a sense of freedom. Frameworks filter variables, hide them, or highlight them at certain times. The interaction of variables causes all sorts of things to occur.

As we age, we can't help but view existence through the many frameworks of our life and death, regardless of whether we call them aging, social science, religion, spiritualism, naturalism, super-naturalism, constitutions, or voodoo. Where does human life begin and end? At the level of the gene, the cell, the individual human, or society? If we alter the frameworks by extending life, what will happen to the balances we strike? What variables should we consider and what should we ignore?

Real death—hard cold disintegration of the molecules that form our bodies and our minds and permit us to think and feel—truly scares the hell out of us. As Heidegger argued, we forget the mystery of life by attempting to capture and master existence in the artifacts of reason.[9] On the one hand, we all want to experience the beauty of life. On the other hand, none of us wants to live in slavery while our bodies fall apart. So which is scarier: a long life in a virtual prison of an aging body, or death? Which, then, is better: a qualitative shorter life, or a longer more decrepit life?

I've noticed that people form an instant opinion of the questions. Some so fear the emptiness of death that they feel any life is better than no life. Others, usually those who believe in an afterlife, live a better and less fearful life on earth knowing that something good awaits them (especially if they behave). This is ironic because science and positivism find religious tenets the opiate of the masses who willingly accept misery to obtain entry into paradise. But thinkers like Jung recognize that death frightens non-religious people so much they cling to a wretched life filled with pills and wires. Science has become a substitute religion—and when it fails to save us, as it eventually must, some of us have nothing to fall back on.

I haven't included every good thinker in this essay, but I have tried to include a sampling of those who have contributed something to the debate. My own view, after spending the last three years on this project, is very simple: we all die sooner or later. We all should live a good life and we all should die a good death. How that translates into specific policies of quantity or quality of life for the young and old I will let each reader decide.

We will see the debate continue.

Mark Moorstein
March 15, 2010

Acknowledgments

Thanks to my wife Susy, and to Kim O'Halloran, Karen Knab, Nadia Rendak, Arkady Cherepansky, Mariam Tadros, and my Princeton roommate Tim Tosta, for their feedback, for fleshing out my ideas, and for editing the many drafts of this essay. Also, thanks to my 92-year-old father, Dr. Benjamin Moorstein, my 95-year-old uncle Saul Mallen, and my 96-year-old mentor, Mozella Carmichael, for providing personal perspectives on living a long life and aging. Thanks to my dogs Casey, Charleigh, Mac, and Hannah, for showing an enviable and sublime dignity when facing death.

The Question of Life and Death

I ask'd thee, "Give me immortality."
Then didst thou grant mine asking with a smile,
Like wealthy men who care not how they give.
But thy strong Hours indignant work'd their wills,
And beat me down and marr'd and wasted me,
And tho' they could not end me, left me maim'd
To dwell in presence of immortal youth,
Immortal age beside immortal youth,
And all I was in ashes.

— Alfred Lord Tennyson, *Tithonus*

Let's assume that the advancing conditions of social organization, medicine, and biotechnology, will carry us a hundred years or more beyond a natural life expectancy, in reasonably good health, but with the burden of minor chronic disease. If life goes on for that long, however, will nature, God, or some faction of ourselves, bolster death to restore balance to the world? Will the super-elderly want to live that long? Because of the potential burdens, will only the elites enjoy the opportunity to super-age—and if so, will democracy and freedom suffer? Will the population weaken physically, mentally and spiritually as it ages? Will the young, pushed out by a flood of geezers, revolt?

In many places in the United States and the rest of the world, the population has doubled over the last thirty years. Rapid growth has brought problems of global warming, a drain on resources, fewer trees and more traffic. Curiously, however, wealth has spread and basic capitalism flourishes even as economies contract. Not only have the young not been pushed out, but life has improved for a great percentage of humanity.

As technology networks spread like veins and capillaries, traditional communities have changed. Some cities have grown, but others have declined as birth and death rates fail to match. New economies topple old balances. Shoved aside by technology are moribund non-competitive cities in which schools and neo-natal wards have shut down and in which nursing homes, pharmacies, and undertakers remain the only businesses that consistently thrive.[10] Pittsburgh, for example, no longer carries its former weight as a manufacturing hub. Better work, cheap transportation, and the internet have encouraged many of its younger residents to move away or change careers. Aging communities no longer command the young to remain—they call out for help, but they have a mournful quality. The more technology seems to expand freedom for some, the more it erodes the life of others.

Population growth as a result of artificially extended lives, and the density of life that almost certainly will follow, has begun to raise new moral questions. Will growth in the geriatric sector contribute to the world? How could immortality—by which I mean "relative" immortality, because to a flea an elephant would seem immortal—not reshape our morality?

To be sure, individual humans can age well, as George Vallaint brilliantly points out after following a group of Harvard students over sixty years.[11] But not everyone goes to Harvard, and very few in the world have the opportunity to lead a life devoid of danger. Only the elites, far more than others, are able to contemplate super-aging without the extensive support of society and intense governmental intervention. But it's the conflict between those who can super-age and those who must support them that we explore.

In a now famous February 2005 article in the *MIT Technology Review*, surgeon and bio-ethicist Sherwin Nuland questioned the slippery slope of a very long life:

> *If we are to be destroyed, … it will not be a neutral or malevolent force that will do us in, but one that is benevolent in the extreme, one whose only motivation is to improve us and better our civilization. If we are ever immolated, it will be by the efforts of well-meaning scientists who are convinced that they have our best interests at heart. We already know who they are. They are the DNA tweakers who would enhance us by allowing parents to choose the genetic makeup of their descendants unto every succeeding generation ad infinitum, heedless of the possibility that breeding out variety may alter factors necessary for the survival of our species and the health of its relationship to every form of life on earth; they are the bio-gerontologists who study caloric restriction in mice and promise us the extension by 20 percent of a peculiarly nourished existence;*

they are those other bio-gerontologists who emerge from their laboratories of molecular science every evening optimistic that they have come just a bit closer to their goal of having us live much longer, downplaying the unanticipated havoc at both the cellular and societal level that might be wrought by their proposed manipulations.[12]

Central to examining the new moral questions underlying super-aging, we must ask ourselves many times who "we" are, or who "we" might become, and what right and wrong means to "us." If we're privileged Americans taking the best and leaving the worst, we certainly will find an answer different from the less privileged. If we're over-extended animals in the biological sense, left to struggle with diminishing resources, we may find an answer that relies too much on human intervention for survival rather than the balances previously provided by Mother Nature and God. If we include the planet in our calculations, our decisions may take profound turns that render our environment hostile.

As thoughtful humans, we struggle to apply morality to science and society. We are unrelenting worriers and innovators. Just as our collective conscience sculpts theoretical morality and codifies rules, our brains struggle to solve practical problems. To understand the future of human existence, we must penetrate the frameworks that harmonize the universe.

In my book, *Frameworks: Conflicts in Balance,* I explore the structure and traits of frameworks. All frameworks, whether cells, societies or moral constellations, possess common features. The framework filters "variables," or elements, like a gatekeeper and establishes boundaries. Frameworks combine, divide, and subdivide. They grow or contract, remain static, evolve or even revolt. To join one, a potential variable must demonstrate some ability to abide by rules. To penetrate a biological cell, for example, a protein has to possess a certain molecular composition.

Within the nearly infinite varieties of frameworks, including those affecting aging, variables can become prominent or invisible, exerting influence loudly or quietly. In the abstract, the freedom of variables, and "freedom" in general, depend on the rules and structure of a framework. Nothing really comes and goes as it pleases—although anomalous things seem to operate under different rules, often invisibly, but paradoxically in plain sight once we know they exist. Bartenders don't have the freedom to steal from drunken patrons—but nevertheless some do. Anomalies usually signal a need to reframe our theories to understand them. Anomalies can pop out of nowhere. They can arrive from space like gamma rays, or mutate from the random shuffling of genes that, like a lottery, allows a human to live a longer or shorter life. Anomalies therefore provide the clues to whether a current framework is unstable. By examining the framework of the super-elderly, we can make predictions about the society that supports them.

My discussion of frameworks aims not at repeating abstract theory. I'm using them to assist in uncovering and predicting moral order—which can emerge in many forms and descriptions, such as regulation, direction, purpose, determinism, emergence, the "invisible hand," or "intelligent design." Frameworks also can provide insight into the right and wrong of perpetuating life.

Unfortunately, the mind can make sense of only so many variables. Even with the aid of computers, an observer's perspective causes him to select and eliminate data.[13] An observer might see all the way down to the atom but suffer an overload of information. Statistical tools may help define relevance, but statistics often miss important anomalies. The behavior of some might suggest an anomaly in others; we might learn of a single quirky tyrant only by logical inference. Thomas Kuhn in *The History of Scientific Revolutions* described the actions of anomalous stars that led astronomers to conclude they weren't stars at all, but planets. Order and disorder play a substantial part in pushing frameworks into different directions. Disorder not only can destroy a framework, it can improve it by forcing adjustments.

The future certainly will produce an environment different from anything we know at the present. Our moral future may affect the form and conduct not just of humans, but all animal and plant life. The changes of life, now appearing as something faster than evolution but slower than revolution, may accumulate the force of an avalanche. By standing back as it plummets, we may predict a likely path even if we never predict everything it consumes.

This discussion will lead us into the fields of science, nature and religion. I have evoked certain writers who have particularly influenced my thinking— the ancient Greeks, Hobbes, Kant, Hegel, Darwin, Freud, Einstein, Jung, Kuhn, Dawkins, Jared Diamond, Fukuyama—to name a few of the many who shape the dialogue of life and death. I don't intend to approach this effort as a biologist or an expert in anything, but rather as a curious bystander visiting this planet for a lifetime. We're all just stopping by for a hamburger and a beer—even if we last for centuries.

Before we begin, let's briefly consider a couple of concepts. First, again, we have to ask who "we" are. As I repeat this question, we (as readers) should consider that "we" can become fluid. "We" can mean who we are now, as we consider these ideas, or who we will become. We may split into rationalists, whom I call "positivists," who trust in the scientific and human mind; naturalists, who seek peace with the visible and subtle balances of nature; and religionists, who believe that spiritual forces, such as gods or ghosts, control the destiny of man and nature. In other words, "we" is a highly relative term. As we use the term throughout this essay, we may jump around, depending on whether we're describing a situation with a universal eye or imagining ourselves within the perspective of groups. One minute we may see ourselves as positivists planning the perfect future. The next minute we may see ourselves hiking a mountain as naturalists, wondering how many other people will live in caves to avoid positivists. And in still another view, we may see ourselves in a religious seminary defending attacks on our spiritual beliefs. I will leave it up to the reader to decide how he or she would prefer to view all of this.

Let's also reconsider the concept of morality. Although we humans have dissected morality so thoroughly that we sometimes fear the term, morality is deceptively simple: it's doing the right thing. Morality therefore overlaps with theology, ethics, laws and duty (among others). But at its core, there can be no moral or immoral action without a context: facts and choices. Even in their most pristine forms, moral hypotheticals presume actors and a stage. Killing, for example, requires a killer and a victim. Killing an innocent in war presupposes a soldier, a woman or a child and a combat framework. Killing a human in peace implies unusual or even radical events.

The framework always becomes complicated, contextual, and something less than universal. If I unconsciously steal bread from an innocent child because some irresistible and invisible force moves my arms and legs, I'm an amoral automaton, indifferent to the gross injustice to the child. It's only when I face a conscious choice that morality enters the picture. If genes and the environment so determine my actions that I lack reason and free will, then morality itself doesn't exist for me. I should be able to live guilt free because I have no alternative to my actions.

But there does exist a natural or universal morality for humans: some things are always wrong. Our religions give us clues about them. Most of us want to employ fairer ways to make choices, to establish a moral policy in a stable system. The evolutionary fact remains that guilt implies sufficient free will to choose right from wrong. We conclude, therefore, that Mother Nature or God has given us an innate morality. As we will see, the conscience has evolved as a tool not only to do right, but to keep us from destroying ourselves by doing wrong.

CHAPTER I

A Long Life

The wise man lives as long as he should, not as long as he can.

— Seneca

To every thing there is a season, and a time to every purpose under heaven: A time to be born, and a time to die; ...

— Ecclesiastes

In lectures and in his book, gerontologist Aubrey de Grey contends that aging is like malaria and other diseases—a scourge. [14] "Old people are people, too!" he argues passionately—aging kills 100,000 people a day. [15] To critics of super-aging who ask how a future society will handle the population imbalance or the resources super-agers will consume, he responds that while the concerns are legitimate, they don't outweigh the merits of saving so many lives and alleviating so much suffering. To those who worry about children and grandchildren who will have to fight to exist and then support the super-elderly decades or even centuries beyond normal old age, he simply casts them off by objecting, morally, to anyone's right to tell a future "speculative" society how to behave.

As one of his supporters maintains:

> [O]ne of the immediate concerns I hear is ... the planet ... running out of resources. Personally, I am convinced that when this problem arrives we will solve it, and that there are a variety of ways that this could be done (much lower birth rates, higher density on this planet, moving into space and/or to other planets), so I am much more concerned with curing aging. I

*don't want to see any more of my friends or family die, and I
would like to enjoy life as long as I want.*[16]

De Grey's (almost Kantian) imperative—to force society to do good
without fretting about the consequences—appeals to our natural desire to
survive far into the future, to experience endlessly the richness of life, and
to continue our journeys toward enlightenment. However, this imperative
indulges those who believe that super-aging is a right. As we will examine in
more depth, such a right presumes social priorities and imposes costs that may
not reap benefits. The right to immortality therefore begs the very morality of
the process de Grey wants to unleash: who deserves the super-priorities and
super-expenses of super-aging?

The consequences of man-made versus natural life-and-death systems are
enormous for the planet. De Grey's laudable desire to alleviate suffering in the
elderly—not by death, but by super-aging—easily could lead to unintended
consequences. For example, if de Grey overrules natural regulation of the life-
and-death system, promoting human immortality in the rigorously controlled
settings necessary to support it, we may not leave our species the flexibility to
cope with environmental events. The natural ability to adapt to disasters may
cease and, in order to avoid extinction, we may find ourselves relying only on
science to save us. If society fails to provide injections, or even the electricity
to power dialysis machines, super-agers could survive for a century or two,
only to die suddenly in droves.[17]

While we may lengthen our lives within tightly controlled environments,
we also could corrupt natural balances on earth—beginning with the strength
of the wider population or the burdens we impose on our children. Perhaps
we may fail to assume adequate regulatory control over nature or ignore, for
mundane political reasons, the innocent and the worthy. Perhaps we may
never control more than a little bit more of our own biological destinies.
How will Mother Nature regard the bastardization of her countless balances?
Perhaps Sherwin Nuland's critical retort to de Grey is right: "[I]t will not be
a neutral or malevolent force that will do us in, but one that is benevolent
in the extreme, one whose only motivation is to improve us and better our
civilization."[18]

We must go farther in our examination. We must examine de Grey's
premise that immortality is a moral right and that the imperatives to extend
life—and not let life terminate naturally—compel us to choose an active
science over a passive nature. If we travel even part way down the road with
zealous immortalists, we may find ourselves assuming the overwhelming
responsibilities that nature and God have appropriated since the beginning of
existence: not only when to give life but when to terminate it.

We feel the dilemma in our guts: how do we preserve ourselves while protecting the human species? Pope John Paul II recognized that the end of life, and its possible extension through science and extraordinary (as opposed to ordinary) medicine, creates huge moral problems. In a 1998 message to an Austrian hospice, he tried to provide guidance:

> [T]he decision actively to kill a human being is always an arbitrary act, even when it is meant as an expression of solidarity and compassion. The sick person expects his neighbor to help him live his life to the very last and to end it, when God wills, with dignity. Both the artificial extension of human life and the hastening of death, although they stem from different principles, conceal the same assumption: the conviction that life and death are realities entrusted to human beings to be disposed of at will. This false vision must be overcome. It must be made clear again that life is a gift to be responsibly led in God's sight.[19]

How long, then, should a life last?

A human life, with ordinary medical care, now naturally lasts seven, eight or even nine decades, assuming good genes, good living conditions and the avoidance of violence. We arrive prepackaged on earth like cars designed by evolution or God or some other force larger than ourselves. We know we should use good fuel, change our oil, wash ourselves and avoid crashing into one another. We don't expect to redesign ourselves from a pick-up truck to a Mercedes, but we can pump ourselves up with the human equivalent of satellite radios or navigation systems or better engines. We can provide ourselves with air bags and restraints. We even can add monitors to tell us when to fill our tires, fix the cooling system and avoid certain routes. We (or our manufacturers) have built in warning systems intended to prevent stupid errors by causing pain.

Competition has forced both us and our cars to evolve in design and function. Efficient engines produce more power using less fuel. Had cars not adapted to the changing demands of travel and competition, we'd still be driving hand cranked Model T's or gas guzzling Edsels. We'd be using oil even faster than today—and eventually we would revolt. No matter how cute the old cars, we would rid ourselves of them in order to make room for the newer and better ones.

What if as humans we figure out a way to keep our old Model T bodies going forever, but with enhanced engines? Even better, what if we find a way to age more slowly, so that we spend far more time in the prime of life? According to biologists like de Grey, super-aging is possible simply by turning off death genes—although "turning off death genes" is a gross oversimplification of DNA control.

In general, cells undergo a process similar to Detroit's planned obsolescence known as "apoptosis," a form of suicide caused when cells no longer function properly. Genes regulate both cell growth and death (i.e. the replication and termination) necessary to maintain homeostasis, or a constant level of cell function in the body. Genes not only trigger apoptosis, but also interfere with it when required. As the body ages, apoptosis itself may malfunction because of damage to the genes, or because something obstructs the pathways from genes to cell function, or because the genes themselves finally quit working. The malfunctions may cause a replication of defective cells or a fatal loss of cells without any replication.

As the ancient Greeks induced the existence of atoms to explain the many forms of material, we look to cells and their genes to explain the many forms of life. Like the car designer with a big trash can next to his desk, death genes evolved to dump bad cells and to produce new models. Early bacteria possessed no death genes at all, but only a few mechanics to repair the cell corpus. Without programmed death, the most basic bacteria died only when confronted by the wrong environment or an enemy. In fact, some bacteria known as Monera live forever in the right environments using relatively simple cell repair, division and replication of clones.[20] As evolution promoted sexual division and the joining of variations of DNA, it introduced apoptosis and the death of the parent as a competitive advantage. By casting aside the parent and test-marketing variations of off-spring, death genes steered a course for the improvement of the species. The best genes survived with the species. As evolution clustered these organisms and formed increasingly complex systems (perhaps through attacks and consumption), the life-and-death system began to favor the strongest children.

While single-celled immortal Moneras still make up nearly half of the life on the planet, humans and every other multi-cellular form of life contain self-terminating mechanisms. Individuals hand off their immortality to the species, allowing the group to survive and adapt with continual additions and deletions. Without natural death or some other default process, older bodies would crowd out their own struggling offspring or replicate obsolete Model T traits by cloning. Dinosaurs still might roam the planet. Complex adaptable life might cease altogether.

As brilliant multi-cellular humans, we may try to interfere with death through science and social control. By reprogramming our genes, reinvigorating the body with stem cell transplants, artificially growing genetic material in laboratories, or just forcing good body maintenance and social conduct, we may stop cancer, heart disease, diabetes and even aging. What then if we succeed?

The question suggests not only new facts, but radically different choices and ways of judging right and wrong. Long life could become so valuable that nothing, even the defense of family or country, would merit a sacrifice. Or perhaps human life could become so abundant that society would demand executions and suicides. The question "What then?" very well could lead to an irrevocable split between those who measure morality from the perspectives of human, or positive law and those who invoke religious dogma. The former thinking may represent scientific and reality-based norms with all of their strengths and weaknesses; the later may embody theology and spiritual norms. Answering the question of "What then?" may reveal a world that humans don't know and wouldn't like. It also may predict a tendency toward genocide in wars fought not just to win, but to kill.

CHAPTER II

Natural Death

I hear the loved survivors tell
How naught from death could save,
Till every sound appears a knell
And every spot a grave.

— Abraham Lincoln

In order to see what lies ahead, we need to ask the biological purpose of death. The natural purpose of the life, of course, is to survive and to reproduce. The natural purpose of death may be to protect the immortality of the species by culling the weakest members.

As evolution takes advantage of available resources,[21] programmed death seizes upon the accidental benefits of death. As we've seen with basic bacteria, a large part of the most primitive life on the planet lives on endlessly through cell division and clone-like replication. The capsules forming the one-celled bacteria have no internal mechanism, no genes, to trigger their end. If these life forms die, some random external thing kills it: climate change, chemicals, absorption by other organisms. There is no such thing as apoptosis, cell suicide, in these single-cell creatures.

Although apoptosis occurs in virtually every multi-cellular creature, the bodies that house the array of cells, or the brains that administer the bodies, possess no upper level function that mandates natural death (with the possible exception of emotion-based suicide in humans). In order to maintain natural population balance, systems actively exploit and factor in random death: bodies wear out or break as a heart stops, a blood clot interferes with brain function, or lungs fail to process oxygen. The body, perhaps belonging more to the species than the individual, unconsciously relies on the basic genetic blueprint to signal death in the event that random accidents and disease fail to kill.

Research into aging shows that after the reproduction period, most genes—again belonging as much to the species as to the individual—more or less give up on the parent. This research has given rise to the "mutation-accumulation hypothesis": genes accumulate fatal mutations at an exponential rate. Dietrich Stauffer explains that "[o]nly the fittest ... dominate in the population [over] time, provided their fitness is inherited and [transmitted] to their offspring. Biological mutations due to copying errors during DNA replication produce disorder, which also can be transmitted to the children. While over several billion years these mutations have [advanced] the first bacteria into better and better life forms ..., over a shorter time scale ... most mutations are hazardous to our health."[22]

But there must be some reason that individual humans naturally live past their reproduction period. Carl Jung suggests that "[a] human being would certainly not grow to be seventy or eighty years old if his longevity had no meaning for the species to which he belongs. The afternoon of human life must also have a significance of its own and cannot be merely a pitiful appendage to life's morning. The significance of the morning undoubtedly lies in the development of the individual, our entrenchment in the development of the outer world, the propagation of our kind and the care of our children."[23]

Many biologists don't buy into the notion that genes give up quickly on individual humans—indeed, as one evolutionary biologist describes them, humans can be "cooperative breeders."[24] Good social conduct may extend individual lives, as George Vaillant in *Aging Well* suggests, not only by avoiding life-threatening choices, but by protecting the slow maturation of children. According to Kristen Hawkes, cooperative "[g]randmothering ... [may] strengthen selection against late-acting ... mutations ... of longer-lived females through the increased reproductive success of their daughters."[25]

Despite all of the medical advances, life beyond the grandmother period hasn't yet increased very much. More people now live a healthier life with chronic ailments, but still generally die at about the same time.[26] More precisely, according to Steven Frank, "From early life until about age 80, the acceleration in mortality increases in an approximately linear way. After age 80, acceleration declines sharply and linearly for the remainder of life. Some of the causes of death [e.g. cancer] also have a lower peak between 30 and 40 years."[27]

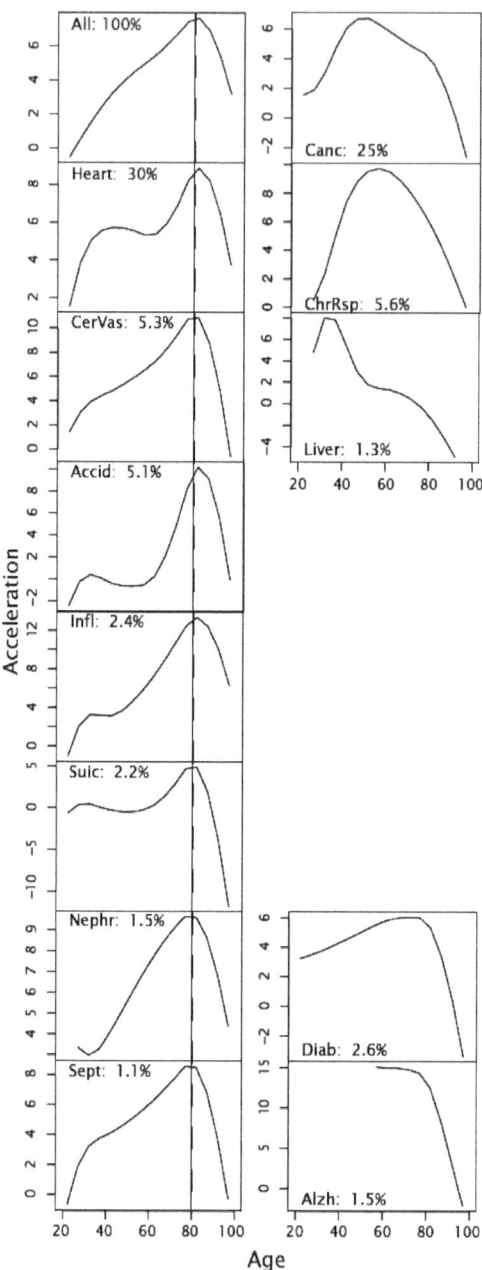

Figure: *Heart* for diseases of the heart; *CerVas* for cerebrovascular diseases; *Accid* for accidents (unintentional injuries); *Infl* for influenza and pneumonia; *Suic* for intentional self-harm (suicide); *Nephr* for nephritis, nephrotic syndrome and nephrosis; *Sept* for septicemia; *Canc* for malignant neoplasms; *ChrRsp* for chronic lower respiratory diseases; *Liver* for chronic liver diseases and cirrhosis; *Diab* for diabetes mellitus; and *Alzh* for Alzheimer's disease. [28]

As Frank explains, "The panels in the left column [Figure] show causes that account for about one-half of all deaths. Each of those causes shares two attributes of age-specific acceleration. ... The panels in the upper-right column ... show causes that account for about one-third of all deaths. These causes follow steep, linear rises in mortality acceleration up to 40–50 years, and then steep, nearly linear declines in acceleration for the remainder of life. The bottom-right column of panels shows two minor causes of mortality that are intermediate between the left and upper-right columns."[29]

Inherent in our construction is the "Devil's Bargain": the erosion and death of cells versus their uncontrolled replication—or trading aging for cancer. In simple terms, aging too far past the grandmother period can't occur because cells reach their physical limits and die. If cells wear out, or can't replicate, they can't defend or repair the body—so self-destruction, or apoptosis, becomes preferable to continuation at an impaired level.

Scientists have noted a number of different mechanisms that cause aging and dying—and nearly all seem to originate in the genes. According to biologists, "telomere erosion," the malfunctioning of "telomerase", and "Hayflick limits," explain a great deal about aging cells and the uncontrolled replication that becomes cancer. Telomeres are DNA sequences that park themselves at the ends of chromosomes. Like a tape recorder that can't play the last part of the tape, a new chromosome can't replicate the entire telomere of the old chromosome when a cell divides. As a result, the new chromosome ends up shorter and lacks some of the old DNA. The missing DNA does little damage until the telomere becomes too short and reaches its allotted number of replications, known as the "Hayflick limit." [30] The cell then fails to respond to instructions to divide. The cell can survive for a time in its non-replicating state, but it begins to lose function: it ages.

Amazingly, however, an enzyme known as "telomerase" can fix the telomeres and extend the Hayflick limits well beyond the grandmother period. The genes that produce telomerase exist in all replicating cells but remain dormant except during fetal development (e.g. in stem cells) and in immune, sperm and a few other cells.

Is telomerase the fountain of youth? Possibly, except that telomerase seems to trigger cancer. Some researchers believe that without telomerase, cancer cell division also would stop at their Hayflick limits. However, cancer cells suffer two simultaneous failures: the first by genetic damage that fails to cut off cell division, and the second as telomerase suddenly overcomes the Hayflick limits. Natural cancer resistance therefore requires aging: the durability of old cells or apoptosis of bad cells before they can replicate. In other words, we can preserve worn out non-replicating cells and decline cell by cell, or we can die quickly by the cancerous and endless replication of bad cells.

Scientists must exert Herculean efforts to stop both aging and cancer at the cellular level. It's even more Herculean, with the millions of variables, to determine how cell termination figures into the larger "emergent" aspects of sociology, politics, ethics, world order, morality, religion and virtually every other framework. The scientific (i.e. medical, biological and social) community provides countless articles on the quasi-genetic, quasi-environmental causes of aging and cancer, including the effects of stress, poor life-styles, diet, smoking, lack of exercise, and so forth.[31] The natural and environmental causes of death not only connect nature to nurture and our individual genes to species behavior, they lead us to larger non-programmed man-made causes of death, such as war, social unrest, or economic deprivation.

Of course, scientists have tracked other "simpler" aging mechanisms that also conspire to kill us—and they have suggested ways to stifle death, again starting at the cellular level. Super-aging advocate de Grey has isolated seven mechanisms, all of which, he is convinced, will succumb to genetic and medical engineering.[32]

Regardless of de Grey's implicit denials of natural death serving any social purpose, natural death obviously performs a difficult, but necessary role, by cleaning up the sickest and most oppressed elements of society, by providing final relief to the suffering and to their overburdened families, by providing term limits on dictators, by balancing resources with the population, and by insuring, genetically, that the healthiest survive. In the short run, and to an individual, there is no question that natural death usually is a monster. We have to look no farther than the starving child or a suffering family member. But in the long run, natural death protects and improves the species.

We know that even without invoking morality, natural death sometimes forces us unconsciously into taking necessary actions. Lemmings, for example, demonstrate that an overwhelming desire for individual survival can lead to wholesale termination. Like all rodents, lemmings breed rapidly in good times and migrate in all directions to seek adequate food and living space— even if it involves mass migration across bodies of water. Their individual compulsive survival instincts (and collective physical pressure from other similarly migrating lemmings) push thousands of them forward, sometimes off cliffs and into death by drowning.[33]

If all lemmings survived without aging or migrating or killing themselves, not only would they overrun competitors, they would overrun themselves. We might as well describe the effect as cancer of the species. The lemming food supplies quickly would give out, their colonies would collapse and they could become extinct before they reached any sort of new balance.[34]

Perhaps the de Greys of the world would pay closer attention to natural intervention (through calamity or otherwise) if they juxtaposed their desires with the patterns of the lemmings. Man's toxic influence on the environment often disguises the cunning power of death. We stare at our potential extinction, but we rarely see it. We understand nuclear holocaust only because of Hiroshima and Chernobyl. Global warming becomes less speculative when we watch the polar ice sheets melt or when an international climate conference hammers a doomsday into headlines.

One victim of cutting the margins too close, too large for anyone to overlook even in death, is the dinosaur. In October 2007, scientists discovered in Argentina the *Futalognkosaurus dukei*, a titan measuring more than a hundred feet with a height of a four story building. As we know, these masters of the world died out because neither they, nor their genes, could adjust quickly enough to drastic environmental changes. [35]

Freud, in his classic observations about the forces of life and death, compared the power of existence with the power of destruction: if entropy—the destructive strongman of nature—causes things to fall apart, it takes an equally strong (or stronger) partner to bring things back together.[36] (In effect, as Stephen Hawking has observed in physics, the fact that we're here means that something went right.[37]) Conversely, if the life force works too well by producing too many cells or too many bodies, the death force eventually kicks in to maintain balance. As lemmings and the *Futalognkosaurus dukei* point out, number and size don't guarantee success. We can experiment with life forms, but the life-and-death system won't let us mess too much with Mother Nature. The forces of life and death are both strong and not easily deterred.

Because of their balance, life and death have become allies rather than enemies. Pope John Paul II correctly sees them as "sister life and brother death."[38] The evolutionary purpose of the partnership must have been, and continues to be, an overall gain from their alliance. Draining life from an old or damaged cell obviously doesn't benefit the cell, but it does aid other healthier cells and the larger body to which it belongs. Likewise, the death of an old and damaged body serves the life of the group to which it belongs. New and improved individuals replace old and weak ones to revitalize the group. The benefit to the individual, existing temporarily as part of a larger group, lies not just in its own natural health to promote procreation, but in its "altruistic" ability to improve others in the group. As humans, for example, "something went right" with us only because of the collective sacrifices of our ancestors.

As with the *Futalognkosaurus dukei*, things don't always go right. Sometimes species become extinct because they can't adapt or reproduce in their own environment or can't move to a more suitable environment.[39] The hallmark of de Grey's immortality is stasis—durability in the face of outside change. The hallmark of species immortality is flexibility and mobility.[40]

Death, whether accidental or intentional, remains only one element of a complex evolutionary invention. The life-and-death system has become a family of (a) random disasters and cell entropy (i.e. processes that break down and fail), (b) the strong life forces necessary to overcome random disasters and entropy, and (c) Mother Nature's regulatory forces behind apoptosis, homeostasis, Hayflick limits and cancers that achieve balance. Natural regulatory function provides scientists the best doorway into examining the life-and-death system—and the most obvious code to manipulate death. But nature's code also embeds the Devil's Bargain, i.e. the choice either of out-of-control replication, or aging. Turning off natural mortality comes at a high cost: species imbalance and the violent temper of death when the population turns cancerous.

As we try to crack the entire life-and-death code, we rely on natural balance to guide our research. It's inevitable, however, with our reasoning, that some of us will try to wrest all death away from Mother Nature. At a substantial cost, some of us may live nearly forever—or at least until our organs physically fall apart like rusted cars, or we succumb to unforeseen disasters. On the other hand, we humans may kill ourselves long before nature does.

How we *should* regulate life-and-death will erupt as the primary concern as science advances. Whether we should totally scrap our body's natural system (including its adaptability), or whether we should try to control all facets of our environmental systems of war, violence, and suicide, are items for intense debate.[41] If we eliminate from the social equation all forms of natural death, our moral frameworks must adjust to new man-made challenges. If we start down the path of total reliance on science and positivism, we may reach a disturbing point where we have no choice but to put Mother Nature in a nursing home (along with billions of others) and enlist humans to kill in order to maintain population balance.

We will need some truly intelligent regulation to mesh genetic micro-systems with the forces of social macro-systems. If we terminate natural death by reprogramming the genetic code, we very well may embrace the worst of our present society to provide death: psychopaths, the unstable or the careless. We may come to view wars, murder, violence, genocide, suicide and abortions as necessary evils—delegated to a class of executioners. In effect, we may look kindly on an angry Malthusian environment to maintain population control.

So, a severe cost will follow eternal cellular life out of the gate: the substitution of all-pervasive human choice for natural selection. We humans, with all of our science and politics and our desire to eliminate pain and suffering, still will have to choose whom to kill and whom to let live. We can only imagine the Kafkaesque rules, organization and people that may contribute to these decisions.

CHAPTER III

Individuals and Groups

All mankind is of one author, and is one volume; when one man dies, one chapter is not torn out of the book, but translated into a better language; and every chapter must be so translated ... As therefore the bell that rings to a sermon, calls not upon the preacher only, but upon the congregation to come: so this bell calls us all ... No man is an island, entire of itself ... ; and therefore never send to know for whom the bell tolls; it tolls for thee.

— John Donne

It's not difficult to compare the "moral" codes of cellular organization to aging human societies. Life constantly balances individualism with collectivity—if only to promote the fittest in both. Individualism carries the benefits of randomness and novelty; groups conserve the advantage of law and predictability. Because survival of the whole depends on a balance of novelty and predictability, the individual and the group must look after one another. Indeed, the group depends on the energy of the individual. When one deprives the other of energy, life of the whole deteriorates.

Individuals and groups each deserve special consideration in probing the morality of immortality. A society remains statistically young and healthy only through the introduction of children and the elimination of the frail—and this occurs one individual at a time. The individual certainly depends far more on the group than the group depends on any one individual, but clearly the individual is essential.

The availability (or lack) of steady resources—e.g. food, or shoes and socks in the winter—has forced all species to create communities of interest. For vultures, it's easier to share a carcass than fight; for humans it's easier to buy a car than to build one. Like atoms without molecules, or cells without bodies, modern individuals can't build outside a community, if only because individuals depend on others to organize and supply resources.

The tension between the sort of individual freedom that we all want to preserve as we age, and group security, runs through every framework. If we look again at the most basic individual, the prokaryotic (non-nucleus) one-celled Monera, we see that it lives as free as anything and never dies. Compared to advanced forms of life, the Monera is virtually nothing—and yet it still connects with a loose community of other simple cells that operate in patterns. The most primitive groups arrange themselves in a sort of ordered disorder, conserving the randomness of individualism in loose organizations. Only as cells evolve do centralized organizations, which demand more energy and complexity, also evolve to provide predictability and regulatory control. Simplicity promotes freedom; complexity limits it. Somewhere between size and shape we find a balance of freedom and security—even when it involves the elderly.

A highly complex clump of cells, such as the body of man, exists not because God or DNA specifically told man to form himself, but because his evolving cells couldn't function otherwise. His body, and other bodies like him, congealed into ever larger cultures, and then formed cities and nations—again because survival and competition drove them all. Man functions both randomly and systematically, from biological local administration (employing metabolic systems, cell apoptosis, replication and the brain) to sophisticated and symbolic regulatory control by groups (such as the family and city hall). Behind it all, the life-and-death system, locked into the genes, transmits not only the blueprint of every cell, but the broader purpose of every society: to strike a balance between the forces of order and disorder, between existence and termination.

Steven Johnson describes the organizing process as "emergence." He cites the behavior of slime mold, an amalgamation that

> *spends much of its life as thousands of distinct single-celled units ... Under the right conditions, those myriad cells will coalesce ... into a single, large organism, which then ... crawl[s] across the garden floor, consuming rotting leaves and wood ... When the environment is less hospitable, the slime mold acts as a single organism; when the weather turns cooler and the mold enjoys a large food supply, "it" becomes a "they." The slime mold oscillates between being a single creature and a swarm.* [42]

Animate, or even inanimate, units often work together to produce a collective brain. The organized complexity allows elements to function more efficiently and strategically than a random assortment of parts. A certain type of self-regulation—nearly identical to what we might call purpose—emerges as the system endures. Dumb systems combine and fall apart as life begins and ends, and as complex organizations add and subtract elements for efficiency. A system effective for one segment of society may mutate as the segment ages.

Emergence theory goes a long way toward addressing the apparent purpose, and even the sentience, of social systems as they evolve from a loose collection of individual parts. In a May 2009 article aptly named *The Coming Superbrain*, the *New York Times* reported, "The notion that a self-aware computing system would emerge spontaneously from the interconnections of billions of computers and computer networks goes back in science fiction at least as far as Arthur C. Clarke's 'Dial F for Frankenstein.' A prescient short story that appeared in 1961, it foretold an ever-more-interconnected telephone network that spontaneously acts like a newborn baby and leads to global chaos as it takes over financial, transportation and military systems."[43]

Perhaps emergence theory can help us predict the evolution of a society in which large numbers of super-elderly come together, but the second law of thermodynamics also provides an explanation: entropy, or the tendency of things to fall apart.[44] The general theory goes something like this: Every system tends to move to disorder, its energy becoming available at lower levels of work until the system becomes totally random and no useful energy is left.[45] To counter entropy, or death, life needs some way to collect, store and convert energy and then use it for non-random and more complex purposes (i.e. to build). Simple cells, which first collected, stored and converted energy through creative anaerobic chemical reactions, eventually evolved, developed nuclei, DNA and something like a purpose (i.e. to survive). Ever more complex organizations, such as bodies, likewise required the storing of energy and the fine-tuning of an operating plan to achieve survival. To the extent that any organization functions at all, therefore, it implies availability of energy, order and, of course, a will to survive; to the extent it fails to function, it implies chaos and a loss of will.[46]

These principles will apply to the super-elderly as they emerge from the general population: they need energy, structure and a will to survive.[47] Deer and antelope may play in some haphazard form on some random plain, but their behavior reveals a mentality and orderliness not entirely different from hungry senior citizens spreading through an all-you-can-eat restaurant.

The process of disorder and decay is by no means all negative. By releasing energy to the group, the death of a spent individual can have a beneficial purpose. In fact, in the case of yeast, one study found that old cells, which can harm the group, induce self-regulation through suicide and supply life to the remainder of the group.

> *Various microorganisms tend to cluster together to survive nutrient depletion, forming multi-cellular communities called biofilms. In such a social community, the benefit of a cellular suicide program seems evident. The self-destruction of virus-infected, damaged, and old cells, which consume dwindling nutrients or spread an infection, contributes to the viability and reproductive success of healthier members of the community harboring similar genomes.[48]*

Groups, lacking a brain as we know it, naturally evolve (perhaps through trial and error) to protect and eliminate their own for the greater good—almost as if, without the free will of a sentient being, they have some innate moral code. In small groups, everyone is family, so everyone benefits from good selection. In a complex body, where cells may live far away from one another, and perhaps share little affinity, selection becomes harder. Cells do what nature has demanded—survive—regardless of the greater group consequences. There, regulators of the larger group must become specialized and more determined to check the havoc of a distant deviant cell (such as a cancer) before it wreaks widespread damage. If a cell, like a serial killer, goes on a local rampage that threatens to spread, the hit-squad of apoptosis has to eliminate it before it kills the body. As Büttner *et al* observe in their article on yeast:

> *Disruption of the apoptotic machinery ... only initially results in a better survival of aged cultures. An aged ... mutant strain is no longer able to re-grow when nutrients become available after a period of starvation, leading to a population with a high percentage of damaged and old cells. In the long run, aging yeast populations benefit from early apoptosis with strains that initiate early death, outlasting long-lived mutants in competition ...[49]*

If only detached individuals occupied the world—whether young or old—families and cultures would never form and group morality would never become an issue. Instead, as Thomas Hobbes argued in *Leviathan,* man in his "natural state" would confront danger and violent death by himself and would use any resource in his defense. Individual man would claim everything and become the aberrant cell always poised to damage others. Because resources are finite, he would wage a *bellum omnium contra omnes*—a war of all against all. Life would become "solitary, poor, nasty, brutish and short."[50] Hobbes might have suggested that our telomeres would never time-out because early death from violence or disease would short-circuit them. There would be no elderly.

Political freedom and moral restraint grow out of the balancing processes of individuals and groups. Groups make decisions as an extension of basic life and death, with their order and disorder. A good decision expands the power and life of a group; a poor one results in a diminution.[51] One-celled organisms, and perhaps arch-individualists, remain disordered only as long as no common purpose calls. When asked if he belonged to an organized political party, Will Rogers quipped, "I'm not a member of any organized party, I'm a Democrat." If the events of September 11, 2001 provide any indication, the most I-am-too-an-island individuals will act in a coordinated fashion and will sacrifice themselves for the greater good when a common danger looms. Common purpose often transforms an organization without any outside motivation at all. Most people don't really know where a party platform steers a party, just as lemmings go about their business without an express order that says, "In two weeks, it's time to jump off a cliff!"

Social positivists want to conquer nature, to use the rational mind to overrule the messy (and lengthy) trial-and-error mechanisms of evolution. As humans survive for longer periods, however, they will generate their own peculiar order. Positivists, at best, will apply an ordering mechanism to nature—but through social evolution, trial and error, they will make mistakes that disrupt the complex and often hidden growth processes tested over millions of years. To avoid social disorder, death and decay, social positivists must construct elaborate systems to dole out benefits and reason. But disorder sometimes serves the essential purpose of transferring energy to the rest of society—and disrupting the supply line easily can disrupt the life of society.

A complex and rational society needs freedom and disorder as much as law and order. So it's not clear how a positivist society will grow and adapt by overprotecting the super-elderly against nature. A totem pole orthodoxy may minimize disorder—but it, like every other living thing, actually needs the random creative energy of nature. In the overall scheme of things, the disorder of nature that incorporates death, serves a critical social survival purpose. Like the accidental organisms that first were consumed by and contributed to the construction of complex bodies, independent variables provide grist to a hungry mill. Without the creativity, randomness, and energy a natural individual brings with its will to survive and its sacrifice for the greater good, future societies may never rise more than a foot off the ground.

CHAPTER IV

Too Much

In the last 200 years the population of our planet has grown exponentially, at a rate of 1.9% per year. If it continued at this rate, with the population doubling every 40 years, by 2600 we would all be standing literally shoulder to shoulder.

— Stephen Hawking

Like many great scientific achievements, the world will note the erosion of natural death not as a headline in the *New York Times*, but as a footnote in a scientific journal.[52] It will take time for us to comprehend the magnitude of immortality because it won't occur on any one day. Each breakthrough in apoptosis, mitochondrial disruption, cancer or telomeres, will accumulate until we wake up day after day and realize we aren't dead.

Long before we fully appreciate life at age 300, we may reconsider the possible mistakes of a brave new world: the cities of the planet may expand into one another, global warming may provide vacation beaches in Alaska, forests may fail with overdevelopment, nearly half the plants and animals may show signs of stress and disappear as we look for new ways to feed ourselves. Land may become so necessary for our long lives that protective monopolies preserve it from the *nouveau vivant* and outsiders of any stripe or color.

Obviously, if more people live than die, the population must grow. Unchecked population soon will remind us of unchecked cell multiplication in the body: cancer. Eventually we will realize that this super-sized cancer will destroy the planet as surely as a direct hit by an asteroid.

If the planet is our collective body, are we silently steering ourselves into a collision? Most discussions of overpopulation address the issue from the framework of improved healthcare, disease control, peace and prosperity for all, as if overpopulation had minor consequences. Does the world truly care about everyone? In fact, we view overpopulation affecting the unwashed masses "out there" differently than ourselves.

"We" therefore will never overpopulate—only "they." Without a referee, survival may pit privileged individuals against the group. If only the elite can live, and live well, will the poor masses not rebel before they perish? But if we slow death for everyone, aren't we tacitly approving the consequences of overpopulation? Perhaps we can hope that we're just steering the life-and-death system to a new and improved balance—perhaps turning the thermostat from a cool 60 degrees to a more comfortable 72 degrees. Or perhaps we're killing ourselves in novel ways we're powerless to see or prevent. Why, we have to wonder, are we acting so contrary to our ideals—or so ignorantly?

Two answers should surprise no one at this point: (1) the biological mechanisms that push us to survive, also push us to reproduce regardless of such mundane consequences as overpopulation; and (2) by taking the brakes off the natural limiting mechanisms, we careen down a slope that has overwhelmed our steering wheels.

A mere fragment of the vast literature on overpopulation reveals two adamant sides. The sky-is-falling side frets over every possible effect of population growth and urges draconian measures to take us back a thousand years. The other side, the head-in-the-sand side, blithely denies that overpopulation is—or ever will be—a serious problem and goes about advocating a world of Methuselahs[53] and large families, over-consuming resources for personal pleasure and leaving the problem of too many people for the next unsustainable generation.[54] Confounding both sides, birth rates have declined in industrialized countries that extend lives through better healthcare and social management, leading not to larger populations, but to smaller and older ones that try to protect both the elderly and the young.[55] The extremes illustrate Aristotle's admonition of "all things in moderation": there's a lot of middle ground to stomp on.

So what really is overpopulation? According to basic definition, overpopulation occurs when the density of life exceeds its supporting resources. To remedy the problem, one needs only to decrease the density or increase resources. Simple solutions—but how?

For millions of years, nature has balanced density with resources by regulating the life-and-death system, or rearranging available space by resizing organisms and forcing migration. As biologists have observed, organisms that reproduce quickly, die quickly—or, like lemmings, they spread out (if they can). Salmon spawn in rivers by the millions and then swim to a vast sea, with lots of resources, where they live for a finite period. Those that survive struggle back to their places of birth, spawn another generation, and then die. As long as the right number of salmon spawns, their population remains stable. However, in some places excessive fishing and climate warming have damaged salmon stocks to the point that not enough return to reproduce.[56]

Small organisms obviously require less space and fewer resources than larger ones—and they therefore reproduce at a faster rate. Larger ones may produce fewer offspring but they generally live longer.[57] In all species, it seems that nature has imposed a million balances to size populations to the environment. The two most important factors in the balance are reproduction, with its variety, and death, with its verdicts of adaptation to changing environments.

Thomas Malthus first expressed in 1798 the concern that humans, freed from the "powerful and obvious checks ... [of] moral restraint, vice and misery" will procreate beyond their resources. Profligate behavior inevitably invites "war ... plagues, violent diseases and famine," forcing Mother Nature to reimpose balance—as Malthus observed when he referred to population "oscillations" or a "spring loaded with a variable weight." [58] Although Malthus' specific calculations of humans versus their resources have proved wrong, his concept has become a compelling doomsday scenario.

Jared Diamond observed in *Collapse* that civilizations fail when man pushes his luck in good times without developing adequate margins of error for the bad.[59] If people impose no internal boundaries on themselves, nature eventually will. Despite exponential improvements in food production, starvation still occurs where distribution breaks down. Disease occurs in close quarters where bacteria and viruses spread. Wars break out where people compete for limited resources.

Paul Erhlich, in his 1968 classic *Population Bomb*, analyzed the goal of "zero population growth." He compared birth rates with death rates and easily predicted that if birth rates exceed death rates, a population will grow. But he also pointed out that even with high birth rates and low death rates, death rates eventually have to reach equilibrium—because people don't live forever. Some demographers have predicted ZPG in industrialized nations sooner than later because kids are expensive and parents don't need as many for labor or security. Others have gone farther, however, and shown that populations themselves age as a function of the birth and death rates. High birth rates and high death rates produce younger populations; low birth rates and low death rates produce older populations.[60]

In 2002 in Madrid, the United Nations sponsored its second conference on aging. Among the findings, the assembly reported the following:

> *Average life expectancy at birth has increased by 20 years since 1950 to 66 years and is expected to extend a further 10 years by 2050. ... [T]he number of persons over 60 will increase from*

about 600 million in 2000 to almost 2 billion in 2050 and the proportion of persons defined as older is projected to increase globally from 10 per cent in 1998 to 15 per cent in 2025. The increase will be greatest and most rapid in developing countries where the older population is expected to quadruple during the next 50 years. In Asia and Latin America, the proportion of persons classified as older will increase from 8 to 15 per cent between 1998 and 2025, although in Africa the proportion is only expected to grow from 5 to 6 per cent during the period but then doubling by 2050. In sub-Saharan Africa, where the struggle with the HIV/AIDS pandemic and with economic and social hardship continues, the percentage will reach half that level. In Europe and North America, between 1998 and 2025 the proportion of persons classified as older will increase from 20 to 28 per cent and 16 to 26 per cent, respectively.[61]

Demographers also have predicted that countries with low rates of birth and death will stabilize sooner—but unfortunately, if super-aging takes root, fewer and fewer children will have to support more and more great great grandparents. The process has already begun:

As almost everybody lives ever longer, a reasonable supply of young people is needed to counterbalance—and fund the pensions of—a growing number of older folk. In fact, fertility rates have dropped steeply in all [Western European] countries in the past few decades from an average of 3.2 children per woman in 1960 to 1.6 now. The rate needed to keep the population stable (assuming unchanged mortality rates and no net immigration) is 2.1. According to the UN's latest population estimates, fertility is currently below replacement level in over 70 countries, which account for nearly half the world's population. But even in the remaining, poorer, half of the world, fertility rates have come down spectacularly, from 5.2 in 1970-75 to 2.6 now. This has been the most important factor by far in the aging of populations around the world.[62]

If population strength, necessary for competition and survival, depends on an average age that ensures enough replacements to support the super-elderly *and* controlled reproduction *and* adequate resources, it would seem that very young and very old populations will compete poorly against populations of moderate age. This suggests that the most competitive populations will settle on birth and death rates neither too high nor too low.[63]

In light of potential imbalances in birth and death rates and the potential weakening of populations, the knee-jerk choice only to limit births rather than discourage long life seems expedient. Although birth control offends the fewest people able to voice any objection, the control of population exclusively through birth rates relights de Grey's fire regarding the social duty to the elderly. How far beyond a natural limit *must* we extend life?

The UN Madrid Report advocates a shift of resources, and therefore world economies, to protect the elderly—but it and other analyses don't believe that a debilitated life should extend infinitely at the expense of society.[64] Still, at least one ZPG group seeks to improve the quality of life for everyone, including the elderly, and finds odious any sort of "capping the life span." It prefers instead to stabilize population "via eliminating unintended pregnancy"[65] rather than focusing in any way on the effects of an extended life. The subtext of its position—which seems to adopt de Grey's line of thinking—is that refusing to prolong the lives of the elderly is the moral equivalent of killing them.

"Eliminating unintended pregnancy" is, however, no different than "capping the life span" of fetuses. The argument implies that if we're willing to terminate "unintended" pregnancies, we would make more space and resources available for "intended" humans. But here there must be some sort of bell curve at work. If we bear too few children, whether intended or not, the population will age and the quality of life will deteriorate. If we bear too many, the population will grow too fast with all its resource problems. Is the population's "intention" therefore the balancing factor—that if stable families merely "want" children, the population will reach the apogee of the bell curve and quality for all will improve?

In her controversial book, *The War Against Population*, Jacqueline Kasun asks "What is an 'unintended' pregnancy? … [T]he words 'unwanted', 'unplanned', 'unintended', 'born out of wedlock', and even 'conceived out of wedlock' have for years been used interchangeably, without definition, and in the face of repeated protests. An unintended pregnancy rarely results in an unwanted child, nor does a pregnancy conceived out of wedlock. The fact that at present an estimated 98 percent of unwed mothers keep their children, despite the demand for adoptable babies, surely suggests that few babies are unwanted."[66]

Moral debates over birth control, abortion, euthanasia and the financial effects of the baby-boomers as they age have sparked mob-like reactions.[67] Mass death of either the young or old as a response to overpopulation immediately casts doubt on the sanctity and equality of an individual's right to life. Genocide, growing out of class, represents a complete failure of morality.

Nuland's article on de Grey highlights the recklessness of both the ZPG'ers and the immortalists in targeting only the unborn for population control. If 30,000,000 otherwise naturally-doomed elderly individuals each year have a greater social "right" to life than 30,000,000 naturally-entitled fetuses, one generation of human life not only pits itself against another in a positivist society, but wages war to weaken the entire population. De Grey's assertion, of course, presumes more than slight narcissism: if any individual life, or a generation, always prevails over the collective life of society, then in addition to the normal restraints on government—life, liberty, speech, religion—we not only have to keep the state's hands off the people's right to survive, but saddle it with the affirmative duty to fight nature to make the people survive. It's a tall order for even the most powerful nation on earth—and an expensive one if it has to provide for each and every individual who demands society's resources. It means that government must become even more pervasive than we imagine. The Hobbesian social contract may come to read: "The party of the first part, whether born or not, in order to allow the government to promote all life all of the time, delegates all freedoms to it; the party of the second part, the government, in order to preserve and promote all life all of the time, assumes all of the rights and duties of the party of the first part." This, it seems, is the definition of totalitarianism.

Although the 2002 UN Conference in Madrid was utopian in protecting the elderly, it's a safe bet that any sane government neither will fight for, nor ever permit eternal life for any individual if the price is impairment of society. Some sort of moral restraint on super-aging is necessary if the world wants balance, and localized societies want to avoid morphing the Four Horsemen of the Apocalypse into four billion new killers.

We all can agree that the necessary adjustments of birth and death rates will occur in some combination of human morality, purpose or just plain survival of the fittest. How supple the balance becomes between population and the resources of earth is anyone's guess—but a human intention, or desire, yet another form of social purpose, seems little more than chest pounding by positivists.

CHAPTER V

The Devil's Bargain

You load sixteen tons, and what do you get?
Another day older and deeper in debt.
Saint Peter, don't you call me, 'cause I can't go;
I owe my soul to the company store...

— Merle Travis

Until Obama, politicians routinely refused to grant scientists adequate federal funding to experiment with animal cloning and stem cells. Moral concerns have slowed the liberation of the genes. Many on the religious right see unlocking the genetic code as original sin: we shouldn't peer into the eye of God and ask him to blink.

We witness the hysteria of both sides of the genetic engineering issue: scientists and medical researchers lobby to enlist the unused stem cells of the newborn to improve the lives of the living and the desperately dying. Religious conservatives react by underscoring a fear that the manipulation of "innocent" cells violates divine law and pushes us toward human cloning or organ farming. Both sides are right and both are wrong.

Moving forward on genetic science means saving millions of lives, improving the lot of the world, and curing hundreds of intractable diseases. Who could object to eradicating diabetes or heart disease? Who could protest better food production or better drugs? Clearly, if super-aging people had the slightest assistance from genetics, they might live without dialysis or pacemakers, and they might become as productive as in their younger years. If we follow the improvements to their natural conclusion, they lead to longer and more pleasant lives.

Or do they? Perhaps longer lives will lead to crushing populations who want a piece of the endless pleasantry. If the quality of life relates to the quantity, not all life for all people can become long and full of happiness.

Even if life continues to improve for some, or even most, many will find it unbearably difficult. But even with the risks, why shouldn't we strive for an unending Garden of Eden for as many as possible? Why shouldn't a Peruvian farmer have the same opportunity (or even right) to super-age as a Queen Elizabeth or Bill Gates? Aren't we all equal? Didn't God make us too?

Immigration presents a guilt-provoking lesson regarding the limits of our principles. A century ago, the Statue of Liberty welcomed nearly any newcomer to the U.S. Our ideals and resources extended infinitely, it seemed. Although many of "us" didn't really like the unwashed masses, we let them into the country anyway: Irish, Slavs, Chinese, Japanese, Africans, Jews and Arabs. These aliens helped themselves by helping us.[68] They provided cheap labor, kept the population age stable, and threaded their way into the American fabric. Nevertheless, the recent flood of immigration has caused us to close the gates because we fear that too many people will degrade our lives. Because we all can't afford the best in food, fuel, medical care, housing and social benefits, we resent subsidizing others. Our self-preservation often conflicts with democratic ideals.

The conflict soon may extend to the unborn and super-agers. The young and old, also competing for resources, already face discrimination—but instead of jobs, healthcare, and housing, the new discrimination will rest on the right to life. Many of us will demand life beyond the grandmother period. Until science finds cheap ways to extend life, however, only a few of us will succeed. As we've seen with $20 million space joy-riders or those who gain an unfair advantage by lobbying Congress, some will bargain hard for admission. No doubt, if the cost of immortality is merely selling one's soul 300 years in the future, many gladly will pay the price. A black market in life may arise in which those with the most money will live the longest no matter how many experts weigh in on character. The criteria for immortality will not necessarily require good deeds.

Eventually, the high cost of body maintenance may give way to Wal-Mart availability.[69] With an efficient market, the cost may decline until almost anyone desiring wrinkle-free skin and a long life can buy them. Computers soon will map genomes quickly, isolate the DNA sequences responsible for repairing cells, and direct the on-and-off switches of cell function. Technology geeks may smack down natural killers faster than Hulk Hogan pinned the Iron Sheik. Geneticists may market Nintendo plug-ins that alter human function.

Perhaps the price of permanence won't present an impenetrable moral dilemma if the markets function efficiently and ethically, and force rational choices by making irrational ones expensive. Perhaps, on the other hand, moral zealots will impede scientific progress to the point that an elongated life becomes a bridge to nowhere. How do we allocate the right, or even the obligation—as de Grey argues—to provide a super-long life in some fair, democratic, and meaningful way?[70] Will we appoint priests, doctors and special commissions to make the moral choices, as we sometimes do with kidney or heart transplants? Will we delegate our material lives to death panels, as Sarah Palin described palliative doctors and age counselors?

The looming clashes beg the basic question of why super-aging—living past a "natural" lifespan—is so important to us. Is it because we fear death so deeply that even probing the issues kicks off existential angst or makes us realize our trivial long term relationship with the material universe? Is it because we fear an eternity of nothingness, as Sartre might ask.[71] Or is it because we have become so addicted to the pleasures of life that, like a house of hop-heads, we feel that our personal needs prevail over everything else? Have we forgotten that life is a gift from God and nature—and not man-made?

The drive for super-aging reopens a framework originally constructed by Christ: "[W]hat shall it profit a man, if he shall gain the whole world, and lose his own soul?"[72] Do we, as super-agers, trade our humanity and our meaning for a long life?

The Devil's Bargain is almost too obvious to state. In one of the most famous and elaborate cautionary tales, Goethe's Faust makes a pact with Mephistopheles. Faust wants to know the world and the devil promises it in exchange for his soul. Faust enjoys lust in super-sized portions, but eventually realizes his folly and seeks redemption by pacifying nature and conflict. When Faust is about to die and give up his soul, God intervenes. Faust wins eternal life—but in heaven and not on earth.

As we repair a cell rather than kill it, geneticists move us closer to confronting the Devil's Bargain. Again and again, we find ourselves trading quality of life for quantity of time. On the one hand, our Fausts may well pacify some tiny part of nature and conflict. On the other hand, if too many bargains occur, they may damn us by unleashing unnatural forces. Stem cells, for example, that provide hope of quality life to the sick often carry the threat of broader destruction, and quicker death, from cancer. Suppressing apoptosis runs the risk of replicating mutant cells. As Nicholas Wade writes:

> *One day … stem cells may help repair diseased tissues. But there is a far more pressing reason to study them: stem cells are the source of at least some, and perhaps all, cancers. At the heart of every tumor, some researchers believe, lie a handful of aberrant stem cells that maintain the malignant tissue. The*

idea, if right, could explain why tumors often regenerate even
after being almost destroyed by anticancer drugs.[73]

On a larger scale, can we resist the Devil's Bargain? If we can tolerate chronic pain, who wouldn't wish for many more beautiful sunsets? If we're in excruciating pain, would we refuse pain-killing drugs even if they shorten our lives?

But even more fundamentally, who brokers these choices? Do we make them at the expense of others? Or do others, at our expense? Should we, after all, enlist panels filled with scientific, moral and political experts, or let the market decide? Immortality may demand more than either authoritarian or market wisdom.

It's one thing to allocate wheat or gasoline. It's another to ration existence. If human intervention truly takes over, will man, neither as god nor devil, know how to administer the immense power he wields? While the moral dilemmas will take generations to explore, the ultimate question, whether we're selling our souls for more time in the material world, already stands before us.

Chapter VI

Rationality and Subtlety

Will you still need me, will you still feed me, when I'm 264?

— Apologies to the Beatles

As the Obama revolution has demonstrated, individuals in a democracy believe they can vote for change. The population theoretically will react to the will of the people by adjusting its conduct until both the individual and society reach equilibrium. But voting for change doesn't necessarily produce change, especially if stasis protects essential population survival. (Witness George W. Bush advocating government intervention to secure the financial markets; and the difficulty of a willing population to establish national health insurance.) In contrast, in a tyrant state without the individual vote, or in a quasi-democratic one in which the vote doesn't extend to the voiceless (such as the debilitated and the children), change nevertheless may occur in some "rational" way because, notwithstanding the government, the population wants to survive. When things go wrong, dysfunction appears in polls or in the streets. In an effort to avoid change, the state may try to isolate or eliminate troublemaking segments of the population.[74] One way or another, however, the population will struggle to survive. If government fails to harmonize with the social survival instinct, the people will revolt, or the society will collapse regardless of the government.[75]

The super-elderly may face the danger of extinction by relying too much on either a social survival instinct that they hope tracks the Biblical admonitions of honoring fathers and mothers, or governmentally supported science that permits super-aging in the first place. Even with offsetting economic benefits, social survival instinct may promote lemming-like reactions that kill large groups if resources become limited. An excessively rational or scientific society, on the other hand, may view the super-agers increasingly as pointless and therefore deserving "special treatment." Whether this sort of "rational" treatment may descend to the immoral Nazi-type *Sonderbehandlung* is anyone's guess, but certainly euthanasia is one often debated alternative to overpopulation.[76]

It may be inevitable, if population segments become too unmanageable, that a society concerned with its own survival will react to marginal members in some combination of rational and irrational ways. Long before the state accepts de Grey's imperative to prolong the life of the super-elderly, society will prioritize the demographics of life and death for its own survival.

Rationality forms the basis of positivism, the ability of man to make wise and moral choices in a seemingly mindless world. The cleverness of Mother Nature, however, could stun a conclave of Nobel laureates, and the moral dilemmas of suppressing her could stump the most Kantian rationalists. Saving a grandmother now at the speculative cost of overpopulation later is rational and moral: it's not even as questionable as heating a room with a lump of coal. The act has little long-term ill-effect and a huge immediate benefit. Still, trade-offs of immediate benefit for later harm set up complex dilemmas: does good sense require us to consider each individual life with regard to its effect on population? Rationality, like Faust, may subdue a natural order that whispers now, but when challenged, roars louder than thunder.

Jung has theorized that humans themselves possess (presumably in their genes) a "collective unconscious," a storehouse of instinct that extends not only to the individual, but also to culture. Religious and other symbols—known as archetypes—manifest and convert this unconscious storehouse of energy into the twins of action and restraint. Jung explains that "religious ideas are associated with parental images."[77] Religions, both overtly and subtly, impose stern commands and restraints: "Thou shalt honor thy father and mother!" or "Thou shalt not kill!" These unambiguous orders, which we seem to know instinctively but don't always obey, have erupted into imperative second person language for each Jew, Christian and Muslim.[78] With regard to living, God hardly needs to explain in Deuteronomy: "I have set before you life and death, the blessing and the curse. So choose life in order that you may live, you and your descendants."[79]

Overt and subtle commands extend far beyond religion. Although few overt codes command that "You shall kill or die for a worthy cause," nevertheless, something subtle and irrational tells us that is exactly what we sometimes must do. Somewhere in our guts, we know that violence serves a deeper purpose—and it frightens us when we articulate it. While we live well and peacefully within defined frameworks, nature maintains its own agenda that includes violent competition.

We therefore know some things no one can teach us and reject others that rationality compels. Assuming we can be largely rational, we note that Kant insists that not only do the ends not justify the means, but that we act now for good without regard to possible bad consequences.[80] Long before Kant, Socrates asserted when faced with death, "[A] man who is good for anything should not calculate the chance of living or dying; he should only consider whether in doing anything he is doing right or wrong—acting the part of a good man or of a bad."[81]

In a tight well-disciplined society, we have to pay close attention to overt cause and effect: if we do something overtly stupid, we pay for it. Advocates of utilitarianism such as Jeremy Bentham and John Stuart Mill, however, view the strict categorical imperatives of Kant as socially unworkable because they disregard larger moral and natural consequences. We have to pay some attention to instinctual drives. Every group that survives adopts self-sacrifice and altruistic death as a worthy means to an even worthier end. Nearly every civilization has developed a warrior class that glorifies death as a way to promote group survival. Military codes plainly insist that a soldier follow a legal order into death—even as society abjures killing. The history of this world is full of venerated acts of murder, suicide and intentional hardship—which we recharacterize as war, altruism, and heroism.

The cold empty universe and the paradise we call planet earth certainly don't depend on human rationality to balance resources. They care little who wins each fight. In fact, man has done almost nothing to improve the earth—and given its inanimate condition, the earth remains silent to the worst environmental atrocities. Whether it can supply the needs and feed an ever increasing population, including a super-elderly segment, remains a question not for the earth, but for those who depend on it.

Still, some believe that the earth does adjust to man's ravages. James Lovelock has gone so far as to suggest that the entire earth is one big interrelated biological and physical balance that will work things out. His "Gaia hypothesis" holds that the earth functions as a homeostatic organism that (to a point) modifies its own environment. One example cites the rising carbon dioxide level in global warming that promotes plant production that in turn converts carbon dioxide to oxygen. Another cites ocean sunlight that encourages plankton growth, which increases cloud condensation and ultimately lowers the global temperature.[82]

Richard Dawkins and Stephen Jay Gould, among others, dismiss the Gaia theory because it irrationally assumes that the earth exercises some intelligent control over resources and populations. The earth rotates passively—and exerts no preference for individuals or species or life itself. Mars does just fine without any life. To Lovelock's critics, the survival process never reaches the whole earth—and it all seems backward with the earth predetermining a goal of natural and social evolution rather than the other way around. However,

Dawkins and Gould would agree that few species live in complete isolation, that the global environment alters the march of evolution, and that the life-and-death system at one level affects the next. In other words, the feed-back influencing emergent levels of cells, bodies, societies, and even the earth may not be exactly rational, but it certainly exhibits an order as it comes to grips with a changing environment—whatever and wherever the environment is.

While environmental balance is basic biology and science, the deeper order necessary to feed and support any population does exist. Aren't all things, including those we can't see or measure, part of the overall balance? Einstein thought so[83]—and so did Buddha, a hundred popes and a million painters and musicians. Genes, cells, bodies, societies, populations and possibly even Gaia herself, rely on detailed and even abstract processes that we, perched in human bodies midway in the emergence continuum (extending even farther from sub-atomic particles to universes), see only parts of even when framed with the right lenses and theories.

Certainly, super-aging will disrupt some of theses environmental and biological balances—but so what? Don't all changes disrupt something? However, if the small rational decisions of keeping a loved one alive (e.g. "all humans are entitled to endless life, my father is a human, and therefore he's entitled to endless life") lead to large disorderly results (e.g. "there are too many non-productive people eating too much food"), something will have gone wrong with the balances. An unstable framework suggests that invisible, perhaps irrational, variables are at work. If instability carries on too long, we expect some sort of framework shift to restore order. A "rational framework" may filter the influence of "irrational" variables, but a haphazard framework shift may push the irrational variables to the surface and leave us in a long period of chaos.[84] Given the deeper order of biology—and the control that DNA exerts on the species when confronted with environmental threats—the exposed anomalies may turn out to be, let's say, dormant genes struggling to express themselves.[85]

Irrationality still seems like randomness or just pot luck—but irrationality, by definition, strips an action only of human explanation: it is "without reason." An action simply may exhibit another order that humans don't yet understand. In the case of biology, we always must consider the behavior of our wily genes as the prime movers of the irrational biological world.

We know that evolution sets the scene for genetic battles: those life forms that compete better, survive better. Someday soon, rational humans, like foreign occupiers dictating fiats, will alter cells, bodies, and society by extending the lives of the elderly with DNA manipulation. Even so, genes faithful to the will of man and temporarily unfaithful to Mother Nature will continue their autonomous evolutionary march, or begin evolution all over again, as if they were mechanical toys reset on their path. Those genes that adapt and survive and adapt again will do so because of their own need to survive. Matt Ridley asserts that genes are always changing, that "eternal chaotic motion could flow from a deterministic system," that there is a "genetic arms race," and, quoting biologist William Hamilton, that there is a "permanent unrest of many [genes]."[86] So human tampering simply will leave man-made and natural genes at different starting points.

Results can vary if initial starting points change—even in the same conditions. "Biological systems are inherently variable, and need to be so to adapt to changing conditions. ... [They] are essentially non-linear and ... not everything can be predicted from a genome sequence. ... [M]uch is left to controlled random integration of cells and systems."[87]

If this randomness holds true if and when scientists reset genes for super-aging, we can expect that natural bodies and genetically-engineered bodies will diverge in a substantial way. Mutating genes may find it advantageous to construct new backs or joints to support the elderly, or restart procreation of the elderly to ensure survival of newly invigorated genes. "In the small scale, deterministic factors are usually dominant ... In the large scale, however, continuous random changes ... move the system towards a critical state characterized by a high unpredictability and sensitivity to small perturbations."[88] "Selfish" genes will use the body to protect themselves. If they are threatened by other genes, they will adapt to protect themselves. They even may destroy one another.

To the rational mind, genes should act like servants of modern man—like iPods or muscle cars. But genes are a product of evolution and don't instantly jump when ordered. "Biological systems are also inherently lazy, in that if a formula works it will be re-iterated again and again rather than expending the energy involved in finding a new solution."[89] In short, genes don't give up their time-tested independence to Johnny-come-lately scientists. As a couple writers explain, "The process whereby organs and entire organisms emerge via natural selection does not have analogies in man-made mechanisms. This would entail, for example, the task of transforming a helicopter into a jet plane by proceeding one small element at a time, with the craft functioning better with each successive modification. Mankind would be inclined to simply design the jet plane from scratch. In nature, however, small random changes can lead to the emergence of complex adaptive structures because favorable systems are built up gradually, with further evolution representing a modification of what has already been achieved."[90] In many ways, therefore, the challenge of the rational mind is how to coax genes into doing what we ask, rather than vice-versa. It really may become competition between "our" genes and those faithful to nature and God. It's Faustian at best.

The "irrational" instinct we possess in our genes easily can conflict with our "rational" need to live in a certain presumed style. It may be irrational, and disrupting to our daily work schedule, to sacrifice oneself by falling off a cliff or drowning—or jumping into a volcano—but we sometimes do it to save our family or society. Instinctual irrationality also can lead to aggression and hatred—perhaps, again, to protect our species. We see existence from only two eyes and don't want anyone or anything to limit us personally—but still we undertake dangerous missions to transmit our genes to the next generation. As Hobbes might suggest, we exercise individual will to buy group insurance for our families.

Population behavior may not seem to connect to our individual conduct—but there is no doubt that unconscious motivations connect both individuals and society. Freud and Jung, of course, used the unconscious to explain much of human and social conduct. A recent study, perhaps demonstrating the effect of the unconscious on politics, has revealed that Americans remained as ignorant of larger issues in 2008 as they did in the 1950's. Yet our voting patterns as a whole appear to provide for our own group safety.[91]

It's difficult to reconcile rationality with instinct, or our reverence for individual life with the overwhelming need to preserve the group. Indeed, we can't reconcile the meaning of our own limited life within the larger population. Although we're part of a cycle of birth and death evident everywhere in nature, we struggle like a programmed rocket to escape the gravity death imposes on our membership in a species. We're afraid of death because we don't really know what lies beyond. And, ironically, our irrational fear of death sometimes brings it closer by ignoring its effect on us.

CHAPTER VII

Religion, Naturalism, and Positivism

... When she has made things so we have to go
Or be wiped out. Will she be asked to show
Us how by rocket we may hope to steer
To some star off there, say, a half light-year ...

The way to go away should be the same
As fifty million years ago we came ...

— Robert Frost, *Why Wait for Science?*

Super-aging will change forever our relationship with God and the universe.

August Comte, the French sociologist, argued in the beginning of the nineteenth century, that in its quest for truth society passes through three phases: theological, metaphysical and positive. Generalizing from history, Comte explained that each phase grows out of the prior one. Before the eighteenth century Enlightenment, religion controlled truth, regardless of reason. With the Enlightenment, man began to assert his natural, or metaphysical rights. As reason prevailed, he entered the final phase, the scientific or positive stage. Positivism, Comte asserted, requires theory, practice and human understanding.[92]

Comte's third phase also states a framework concept of visibility. "If it is true that every theory must be based upon observed facts, it is equally true that facts cannot be observed without the guidance of some theories. Without such guidance, our facts would be desultory and fruitless; we could not retain them: for the most part we could not even perceive them."[93]

Framework theory lets us view Comte's progression in another way. Religion, naturalism and positivism are progressive sub-frameworks of human organization, nested like Russian *matroshka* dolls. Within the overarching universe (defined by one dictionary as "the totality of all matter and energy

34

that exists in the vastness of space, whether known to human beings or not"[94]), religion asserts dominion over everything—both *material* and *spiritual*. (Indeed, the Bible begins with, "In the beginning God created the heavens and the earth. ... [T]he *spirit* of God was hovering over the waters."[95]) By contrast, nature extends only to the limits of the *material* universe (although this may be by definition).[96] Science, as the most nested doll, frames only as much of nature as it can describe with discovery, logic and experience.[97]

Scientists wouldn't even know if they reached the limits of the material universe, let alone the spiritual one, because knowledge, as Plato asserted, is merely "justified true belief," or a process of the mind.[98] As Siddhartha suggested, the universe "is so large that it has no exterior, and so small that it has no interior." The universe reveals itself in doses.

Perhaps we might examine immortality's colossal impact on man's understanding of his universe by asking not just how the extended *presence* of life might affect religion, nature and science, but rather how the relative *absence* of death might. Certainly, as a starting point, if the soul delays in leaving the body, it delays in entering the spiritual world; and a man only reluctantly may deal with salvation or otherwise commit his soul to heaven or hell, nirvana, reincarnation or enlightenment.[99] The Devil's Bargain wouldn't exist unless the devil upped the ante.

Writers have ascribed to religion a myriad of purposes, ranging from mysticism to soothing psychology, community structure and morality.[100] However, most writers agree that religion chiefly addresses the proper conduct of life, salvation and the mystery of death. Take away salvation and death from religion and it's left to deal primarily with material and mundane concerns. Super-agers ultimately will die, but as in filing taxes, most people will put off serious consideration of it until it begins to knock on their door. Still, even if the softest knock doesn't come for centuries, material man must wonder whether he deserves, for his good or bad deeds, a refund or penalties in some eventual day of reckoning. Like the tax man, death doesn't let us forget him completely. Neither will religion.

The reward of eternal peace and the threat of eternal damnation afford religion enormous control over the frightened man.[101] If death becomes too remote, and God's judgment too abstract, humans largely may disregard religion, leaving it not only with less material control, but with diminished moral authority. How will religions react to this erosion if it occurs?

Francis Fukuyama suggests in the *End of History and the Last Man* that religious cultures that resist liberal democracy, with its positivist ethics, laws and technology, are doomed to disappear.[102] A study by the Freedom House notes the anger and defensiveness that some religious sects exhibit when confronted with humanist challenges to its authority:

> *Wahhabi writers feel particularly outraged ... that an entity*
> *other than God ... can make laws for men and women ... In*
> *fact, all systems and political ideologies outside ... a strictly*
> *Islamist theocracy, whether they are democracy, socialism,*
> *capitalism, nationalism, or any other, are rejected as products*
> *of infidel minds and therefore against God and his laws. ...*
> *The entire concept of a civil or positive man-made set of laws*
> *subject to majority approval ... is illegitimate ... because ...*
> *this infringes on God's undisputed sovereignty ...*[103]

However, in June 2009 President Obama delivered a speech in Cairo in which he refuted the inevitability of conflict between globalization, with its humanist values, and religion, particularly Islam:

> *[F]or many, the face of globalization is contradictory. The*
> *internet and television can bring knowledge and information,*
> *but also offensive sexuality and mindless violence. Trade can*
> *bring new wealth and opportunities, but also huge disruptions*
> *and changing communities. In all nations ... this change*
> *can bring fear. Fear that because of modernity we will lose*
> *control over our economic choices, our politics, and most*
> *importantly our identities—those things we most cherish about*
> *our communities, our families, our traditions, and our faith.*
> *But I also know that human progress cannot be denied. There*
> *need not be contradiction between development and tradition.*
> *Countries like Japan and South Korea grew their economies*
> *while maintaining distinct cultures. The same is true for the*
> *astonishing progress within Muslim-majority countries from*
> *Kuala Lumpur to Dubai. In ancient times and in our times,*
> *Muslim communities have been at the forefront of innovation*
> *and education.*[104]

If stressed by the possibility of material immortality, however, the moderating forces of religion may become quirky or Jonestown-like and use man-made death to reinvigorate their own moral purpose. Some religions may view death as an emergency ticket off of earth—like the Heaven's Gate cult that committed mass suicide in 1996. "[T]he planet is about to be recycled, and ... we see ... planet Earth as a steppingstone. Just as with a civilization, that civilization can evolve upwards—each segment within that civilization has the option to become more civilized, less barbaric."[105]

Benign off-shoots of present religions may treat death as an historic footnote to faith—that like ancient Greek culture mainly concentrate on ethics, love and beauty. They may emphasize the benefits of prayer, mind-clearing, charity, and forgiveness that man needs for a very long life. Like some sects of Quakers and Jews, others may abandon fanciful notions of heaven and hell in favor of a moral life built on logic and persuasion.

Some religions may seek reconciliation with the science of immortality by placing it under their control.

> *The problem in western civilization is that science is separated from religion and in some cases it fights religion. We [Muslims] welcome the idea of genetic engineering. It is one of the greatest discoveries of our time and is shared by many countries. ... There are many benefits we can derive from this, say, for instance, in treating genetic diseases by using the effective genes to prevent harm or disease. ... [W]e hope it is used for the benefit of humanity and that its guidelines will be according to the views of qualified [religious] jurists.*[106]

Or perhaps others may bring heaven to earth, like the Hare Krishnas who "propagate spiritual knowledge ... and educate all peoples in the techniques of spiritual life."[107]

In any event, it's unlikely that material man will treat faith and spirituality as completely irrelevant because they offer him peace and serenity on a chaotic earth. Lao Chün explains:

> *If a man is able to remain permanently pure and motionless, heaven and earth both at once will come and dwell in him. The spirit of man loves purity, but his passions cause disturbance. The heart of man loves rest; but his desires draw him into motion. If without intermission he can abjure his desires, his heart will become naturally quiescent; if he can cleanse his heart, his spirit will become naturally pure.*[108]

No doubt super-aging will radicalize faith. Science and faith long have battled one another, sometimes needlessly and sometimes necessarily—and it's likely to continue. Many theologies assert that man can't find truth without a belief in a guiding spirit.[109] Others, like Dawkins, see as essentially nonsense claims about reality rooted solely in personal perceptions that require no testing or peer review.[110] Faith, however, may mean nothing more than a purity of thought or the ability to transcend empirical measurements in finding truth. Science may mean nothing more than pursuit of knowledge in the workings of nature.[111] The entire conflict may lie in the definition of truth, which religions view as less reality-based than science.

But even in pure reality, science will have to examine the nature of death as more than simple termination and with more than just material tools: it already relies on the orderliness of the unseen. "God doesn't play dice," Einstein asserted.[112] Although Pythagoras measured stars with his eyesight and found rational relationships, we can't rely on personal senses to verify the connection between distant stars and sub-atomic particles. In addition to our tools and reason, we must trust an imagination that in earlier times would send us to an asylum. In order to find direction in our exploration, we induce far more than we actually prove. The evolving string theories of physics, for example, predict the existence of additional dimensions—entire universes—that human can't see, but can only imagine.[113] As Einstein also stated, "Imagination is more important than knowledge. For knowledge is limited to all we now know and understand, while imagination embraces the entire world, and all there ever will be to know and understand."[114]

Super-aging, wholly dependent on man's wisdom to tinker with nature, will beg his interaction not only with the orderliness of the material world, but the confusion of the spiritual world. Life and death, by definition, are natural states of "being" and "non-being." If we live so long that we never care about anything but the rational world, we still will wonder.[115] If we exist only in the world of "what is," we will imagine "what isn't" even if it's remote and speculative. There are, in other words, at least two and many more universes: one in which we fly on precision instruments, and others that we have to fly on belief.

The universe we know seems endless and full of life, yet we can't help but wonder what will occur if it too dies. As we look at the stars, the vast unknown stares back, pregnant with possibilities. Even for the Milky Way, we know somehow that death waits patiently. If we spend a million years searching for a place to land in the heavens, we never lose hope that one exists, or fear that it too may terminate. Maybe the Big Bang will lead to Big Bang 2.0, giving us another life on planet Xorg instead of planet Earth. Or maybe it won't.

Mother Nature lights a spiritual fire in the belly, and naturalists marvel at the stars, energetically climb a mountain, explore Alaska, or dig beneath the sea. Neo-transcendentalists urge man to reject an unlimited reliance on science and embrace a simpler nature. They too sense something more than hard cold science in the life of the universe. Unlike Protagoras who believed that man is the measure of all things, naturalists find it difficult to consider man all that important. They regard him as obstructionist, or as only a nano-part of the entire picture.

Despite the trumpets of technology, humans innately fear tampering with their natural or God-given structure. Science learns from trial and error, but most humans have little desire to become the dead guinea pigs of scientific error. Perhaps our spirit—our faith, love, charity, and belief in something greater than life—conserves our trepidation. Perhaps Carl Jung was right when he said that spiritual being was essential to our well-being.[116] While part of us welcomes immortality as an element of survival, part of us remains mortally terrified of the violation of natural law. Even if science figures out how to thwart death forever, death will invoke counter-powers as broad as the universe to invite us to the unknown. We may end up with a choice between leaping onto the cattle cars of immortality or tying ourselves to the tracks to avoid it.

Perhaps the looming conflicts between man, nature and faith, exacerbated by super-aging, will become only issues of perspective. Man won't take over the universe anytime soon; death won't disappear. Man and religion will survive, with nature acting somewhat as a mediator. Living in harmony with nature and with faith in God is probably the best man can do while he struggles with the problem.

CHAPTER VIII

Power, Freedom, and Long-Term Existence

Oh! I have slipped the surly bonds of Earth
And danced the skies on laughter-silvered wings;
Sunward I've climbed, and joined the tumbling mirth
of sun-split clouds,—and done a hundred things
You have not dreamed of—wheeled and soared and
swung
High in the sunlit silence. Hov'ring there,
I've chased the shouting wind along, and flung
My eager craft through footless halls of air...
Up, up the long, delirious, burning blue
I've topped the wind-swept heights with easy grace
Where never lark nor even eagle flew—
And, while with silent lifting mind I've trod
The high untrespassed sanctity of space,
Put out my hand, and touched the face of God.

— John Gillespie Magee, Jr., *High Flight*[117]

As technology extends our lives, it alters our concept of freedom.

Until man's arrival, the history of life has been the history of harmony with nature. As complex life has emerged from a collection of cells, it has exerted only the freedom necessary to survive in its environment—and not much more. But that "not much more" has given rise to the slightest variety which permits evolutionary selection. Incremental freedom continually has expanded through the competitive talents of survival. As a flower blooms brighter, it has attracted more bees to spread its pollen; as a peacock struts its colorful stuff, it has attracted a more ample supply of females for reproduction. As man develops his senses and especially his brain, he has pushed against his

40

natural restraints with tools invented to ease his burden. Successful hunters, farmers and innovators have attracted mates and have survived to lead better and longer lives.

Some traits originate for one purpose but through the exercise of physical freedom evolve into another. Through luck or accident, they provide advantages for survival. Although we've long since evolved from slime mold that uses smell to track down food, our pheromones enhance our memory and our sexual reactions. Our voices, once used for sexual attraction in our more primitive forms (when we were birds and frogs), have become the pathway to sophisticated language, music and abstract thinking.[118] Those painted toes at the end of some hot model's legs may not remind us of our relationship with primates that hung from trees, but they actually have had a purpose. The thumb, a digit freed when proto-man began to walk, has become the key component of manual dexterity and construction of habitat.

Freedom itself has evolved within improving frameworks, and it therefore means something different to modern man than it did to proto-man. It will mean something altogether different to the human who super-ages.

Hobbes wrote in *Leviathan* that freedom is "the absence of opposition; by opposition, I mean external impediments of motion; and may be applied no less to irrational, and inanimate creatures, than to rational. ... [W]hen the impediment is in the constitution of the thing itself ... it [lacks] the liberty ... [and] the power to move; as when a stone lieth still, or a man is fastened to his bed by sickness."[119]

If freedom is the ability to exercise a power without restraint, then it depends on two factors: (1) the existence of the power, and (2) the ability to overcome any restraint on that power. My dog lacks the freedom to make the sun come up at 2 a.m. because, first, despite his healthy bark, he has no power to change the planet's rotation, and, second, even if he had the power, I wouldn't let him use it at 2 a.m.

For man, freedom exists as intellectual (or spiritual) freedom, which permits him to imagine; physical (or natural) freedom, which addresses man's power in the real world; and political (or moral) freedom, which concerns man's social conduct. While animals may experience physical freedom, few animals ever experience the full range of freedoms—and therefore never feel their loss.[120]

Intellectual Freedom

All human freedom begins with the mental health of the individual and implies not only a power to think, but a power to think beyond restraints. In order to understand freedom, one first must perceive. As Aristotle asserted, "[T]o perceive that we perceive or think is to perceive that we exist."[121]

In a healthy body and free society, our five senses and our reasoning empower us to act. We build real, virtual or nano empires; we travel to the moon. Even if we remain paralyzed, our brains can "see" beyond our physical restraints—and we can exert intellectual and spiritual freedom. Albert Schweitzer once lamented that "[t]he tragedy of life is what dies inside a man while he lives."[122] Even trapped within a body, we can imagine, remember and explore the universe. Jean-Dominique Bauby, a stroke victim with "locked-in syndrome," unable to speak or move, wrote with the flutter of his eyelids that we still form pictures that no camera can duplicate, and imagine power we can't exercise. "My diving bell becomes less oppressive, and my mind takes flight like a butterfly. ... You can wander off in space or in time ... visit the woman you love. ... You can build castles in Spain, ... realize your childhood dreams and adult ambitions."[123]

Death's connection with intellectual freedom probably has vexed man since he could think at all. Nearly two centuries ago, existentialist Soren Kierkegaard worried in *The Concept of Dread* that the ability of man to live free, knowing he will die, creates an awesome responsibility unlike animals that simply respond to their nature.[124] The existential angst Kierkegaard had in mind enlarges for those bound to an extended life. The high-maintenance get-your-body-checked-every-day sort of life that de Grey proposes—the near total dependence on others—may not depress the resilient intellectual freedom of a Jean-Dominique Bauby. But if the super-elderly descend into a prisoner-like state with no freedom but their imaginations, many less-robust elderly may wish for death. A century before Kierkegaard, in *Gulliver's Travels*, Jonathan Swift wrote that when the suffering immortal Struldbrugs "see a funeral, they lament and repine that others have gone to a harbor of rest to which they themselves can never hope to arrive."[125]

If we consider, as Hegel once did, the difference between the "is" and the "ought," we as super-agers easily could become envious of the physical freedoms of younger generations.[126] Existentialists say we need finality to define our lives and the possible freedom we might exercise in life.[127] Without death, or some sort of end-point, our lives lack urgency. But what urgency will we feel if our minds fill with fear as death approaches, our bodies become more immobile and we lose our ability to act? If we have no means to execute our dreams, an infinite material soul requires, as Kierkegaard might bemoan, that we assume infinite responsibility for producing purpose and meaning. Our unending intellectual freedom—minds trapped inside aging bodies, more often looking out of windows and imagining things to do and places to go—becomes the real form of slavery.

The concern has plagued the elderly for at least as long as literature has existed. Homer's Odysseus laments:

> *Of mortal creatures, all that breathe and move,*
> *earth bears none frailer than mankind. What man*
> *believes in woe to come, so long as valor*
> *and tough knees are supplied him by the gods?*
> *But when the gods in bliss bring miseries on,*
> *then willy-nilly, blindly, he endures.*
> *Our minds are as the day are, dark or bright,*
> *blown over by the father of gods and men.*[128]

At the very best, super-aging minds will become frustrated and bored with increasingly bad health and immobility. Judith Freeman, in *The Long Embrace*, connects such frustration with the diminishing quality of life illustrated by, of all things, fast food. "Fast food is about estrangement and existential ennui, about loneliness, and boredom, and absence, and an arresting of traditional patterns of family life and social context. Who cares if the meal is inferior? If it gets you out in the world? If it gives you something to do? And the chance of meeting other people." Alain de Botton makes a similar observation, "There must be a reason that French existentialism emerged out of the French equivalent of the fast food joint, the Parisian café... Lonely people smoking Gauloises and keeping warm chatting to each other."[129]

It's in our nature to challenge any barrier. We want to rocket to Mars, envelop New York's Central Park in cloth, smash atoms to determine new particles, earn eight gold medals at the Olympics. Our freedom theoretically grows with each push-back of natural and political restraints. To some extent, any life is free no matter how bad things become—as long as we can think. This intellectual freedom may mean that even at the lowest ebb of human life a "slave in chains is as free as his master."[130] However, tell a tortured prisoner he's as free as his torturers and he may want to reverse roles. Because of the chains, physical slavery is never as free as non-slavery. To the super-aged, bound more by tubes and drugs rather than chains, inevitably limited in physical freedom and unable to participate in the world, social restraints become increasingly irrelevant.

Still, some super-agers gladly may suffer an eternal Sisyphean life because, for some instinctual (or vestigial) reason, the life-and-death system has programmed their minds to survive forever and to use whatever freedom they have. Camus seemed to think that, notwithstanding the absurd task of eternally pushing rocks up a mountain, suicide isn't an option.[131] However, few aging people cheerfully would accept the trials of a Bauby.

Our evolved freedom of thought—imagination—carries us beyond nature and makes us wonder what exists on the other side of life or in the most remote niches of the universe or in the spirit world. It all creates an interesting natural paradox: we are free to imagine life beyond our limits, but not to live it. Perhaps my dog, even with his intelligence, has received a gift in not knowing what to expect beyond his termination. The freedom to think is the freedom to wish—and it is an awesome burden to fulfill.

Physical and Natural Freedom

Death and decay—entropy—are the most obvious natural restraints both on society and on our bodies. Regardless of any kind of freedom, we die. We can't legislate eternal life any more than we can ask a toaster to make the sun rise. Our physiological structure, far more than our thoughts, our relationship with politics, or our ideals, controls our daily capacity to live. "Give me liberty or give me death!" presumes that we have a life to surrender for a principle. What good is the freedom to think or vote if we can't breathe?

Man comes prepackaged with physical powers that afford certain freedoms like running, jumping and swimming. New physical powers and freedom, such as flying, or sightseeing on the moon, however, depend on technology. When man first imagined new tools, new directions and the possibility of soaring with the eagles, he only suspected his potential. He hunted, fished, and farmed for food with ever greater freedom. By current technology, "primitive" man suffered greatly in defending himself and his family against weather and predators; but by his own standards he advanced. He adhered to genetic and instinctual controls, which, of course, selected him as the fittest for survival. He remained tied to an evolving community for the protections necessary to procreate and perfect that survival. He didn't feel a loss of freedom because he couldn't fly an airplane (although he probably admired the freedom of birds) or visit the moon.

Man's technology, borne from intellectual freedom and translated into ever growing physical freedoms, enhanced community survival. Survival didn't favor crazy individuals who jumped off cliffs to imitate birds or wandered haphazardly from their secure environments, but it did reward the inventors of weapons, wheels, and wings. Freedom passed between the individual to the community: a creative society had a better chance of adapting.

Although survival alone allowed some natural freedom, neither man nor communities could afford to flirt too much with fate. Even in times of war, when the human species depended on fearless individuals willing to kill and be killed, groups conserved proven skills. A more refined balance of freedom and restraint developed as a necessary by-product of a collective life-and-death system. As societies developed enough resources to provide a margin of error, leisure, and then, perhaps, justice, broad political freedoms came into fashion. Still, the high cost of breaking restraints prohibited man from asserting too much more risk than necessary for survival.

Because our minds and bodies have natural limits (e.g. we can't memorize every fact or be everywhere), we're inexorably restrained. And getting old doesn't help. Inventions may extend our physical limits, but even with the cleverest technology, our social, political, and moral structure curtails us. Unrestrained freedom may allow us to explore new planets or ski out-of-bounds mountains, but it also can wreak havoc in society—exactly what Hobbes feared.

Political Freedom

Political freedom is a right to think and act in society. According to Ayn Rand, rights "are a moral concept—the concept that provides a logical transition from the principles guiding an individual's action to the principles guiding his relationship with others—the concept that preserves and protects individual morality in a social context—the link between the moral code of a man and the legal code of a society, between ethics and politics. Individual rights are the means of subordinating society to moral law."[132] Political freedom, even for the individual, is hardly unlimited. As Rand points out, "Freedom, in a political context, means freedom from government coercion. It does not mean freedom from the landlord, or freedom from the employer, or freedom from the laws of nature which do not provide men with automatic prosperity."[133]

The exercise of political freedom by the super-elderly means little without a foundation of intellectual and physical freedom. Do you want to fish without a governmental license? If you have a boat and a lake, you probably can fish without offending others. But if you suffer from dementia or you're bedridden, what hollow power does a license convey? Do you want to live forever? If you have enough political power you can buy a permit to live forever—except you still need to overcome biology. It could cost you far more than a permit. The pharaohs, with all their wealth, hardly scratched mortality.

Politics, which examines the decision-making of groups, frames freedom either as the power to overcome authoritarian restraints (e.g. "the king ends slavery"), or the power to rein in government (e.g. "the king wears no clothes"). We commonly note that our American Bill of Rights curbs government rather than grants some super-human power to leap over statutes in a single bound. Political freedom, wrapped in a collective relationship, nevertheless is empowered by individual physical and intellectual freedoms. Political freedom not only constrains governments from tyranny and genocidal behavior, it prevents individuals, exercising their own balance of power, from destroying one another. A million considerations, such as balance, risk, natural ability, and moral restraint, regulate the free and civilized man.[134]

Society often conflates political freedom with physical or natural freedom. To be sure, to the extent that government checks our natural freedom, we become as prisoner-like as the physically disabled. When we're young and strong, laws restrain our physical ability to act: some of us drive recklessly or assault others. Laws sometimes paternalistically refuse to let us sail around the world, as in the recent case of a thirteen year old Dutch girl.[135] As we age, however, our physical limitations inhibit us far more than the government. In our prime, we want and expect government to stay off our backs. In our old age, we ask to government to brace our backs. We seek altruism from government; we desire others to provide for our well-being. As a society, we remain less confident of government's long term goodwill if it restrains our natural prowess, but more confident if it protects us against harm.

Political altruism nevertheless scares us. Ayn Rand trenchantly asserts that "[t]he social system based on and consonant with altruist morality—with the code of self-sacrifice—is socialism, in all or any of its variants: fascism, Nazism, communism. All of them treat man as a sacrificial animal to be immolated for the benefit of the group, the tribe, the society, the state."[136]

American culture ingrains the cudgel of anti-government rhetoric. "We're from the government and we're here to help you" is one of America's most notorious lies. Ronald Reagan admonished us in his 1989 farewell speech that "man is not free unless government is limited. There's a clear cause and effect here that is as neat and predictable as a law of physics: As government expands, liberty contracts." Perhaps, as super-aging expands, liberty also contracts—especially if it depends on government. How could prolific super-aging continue without government support? Certainly the private market will find little profit in large-scale geezer philanthropy.

Friedrich von Hayek explains that a broad definition of the word "freedom" can produce a sleight of hand that turns political freedom for one into economic servitude for another. This suggests—again—that de Grey's moral and economic imperatives to save the super-agers at all costs may disguise a power shift, "freeing" the elderly, but enslaving those who pay their bill.

> *To the great apostles of political freedom the word [freedom]*
> *had meant freedom from coercion, from the arbitrary power*
> *of other men, release from the ties which left the individual*
> *no choice but obedience to the order of a superior to whom*
> *he was attached. The new freedom promised, however, as to*

be freedom from necessity, release from the compulsion of the circumstances which inevitably limit the range of choice of all of us, although for some very much more than for others. Before man could be truly free, the "despotism of physical want" had to be broken, the "restraints of the economic system" relaxed. Freedom in this sense is, of course, merely another name for power or wealth.[137]

It's easy to see that humanity rides a pendulum between the extremes of chaos and social repression. Neither unlimited political freedom nor unlimited governmental restraint adequately balances the "rights" of the super-elderly and society. When freedom for one becomes slavery for another, the social framework devolves into a zero-sum game in which some win only when others lose. The analysis certainly has strayed from the Hobbesian exercise of unlimited natural power, where man can create whatever his talents allow him, and has come to rest within a society that leans toward rationing resources and tries to overpower even physics to achieve a result. Scientists, however, remain Hobbesian in this sense: natural forces, such as energy, mass or time, do far more than government to enable or restrain any object.[138] The laws of man don't extend beyond the laws of nature. Man, like even the universe, wasn't meant to live forever.

In our ever-prolonged struggle against slavery of the mind, body and society, we use what we can. Unless we rely solely on the mind (or spirit) as the sole source of material life—which is yet impossible—we will face physical and political challenges not only in exercising freedom, but in defining it. We don't know what waits beyond natural life, so we don't really want to gamble too much to cross over to death. It may be that in both a material and spiritual sense, we're really just dust in the wind. But in a peculiar way the dust controls the wind: life resists the currents of death, evolves and even builds. Behind every construction is our desire to venture beyond the restraints—which we call freedom—and immortalize ourselves while we wait, somewhat disbelieving, for physical death. Freedom challenges the limitations imposed by mere survival. We trade our work—as one form of self-imposed slavery—for other forms of freedom. We build roads, edifices, and cities, and enjoy art and music. They give us the means, and meaning, to enjoy the time we have on earth and to provide monuments for our children after we go. As everyone seems to conclude, the predestined restraint of death motivates the freedom of life.

CHAPTER IX

Knowledge

Once out of nature I shall never take
My bodily form from any natural thing,
But such a form as Grecian goldsmiths make
Of hammered gold and gold enamelling
To keep a drowsy Emperor awake;
Or set upon a golden bough to sing
To lords and ladies of Byzantium
Of what is past, or passing, or to come.

— William Butler Yeats, *Sailing to Byzantium*

Has science made spiritualism obsolete? If so, what hope do super-agers have as their bodies obey the laws of physics and fall apart? Has science become our religion?

As a junior in a Midwestern high school, I accidentally started an intense debate with my English teacher—and a life-long simmering debate with myself—by writing a theme about the difference between science and religion. I wrote what seemed obvious: that science controlled the known and religion controlled the unknown. My English teacher gave me an F for my efforts, and told me in prolific red ink that everyone knows scientists are religious and theology grasps reality. "Priests still believe in life after death!" I argued in response. My outraged teacher brought the rest of the class into the debate and called for a vote. My class not only voted me dead wrong about who controlled what, but blasphemous to boot.

The Fear of the Unknown

As we age, we turn our attention toward death. What lies ahead? Can we forestall the inevitable? Will death bring us pain, or will we find peace? Will we die a good death, or a bad one? Will we die alone? All of these questions make it seem that we're taking a long trip to a place we don't know. Is it ever possible to preview what lies ahead on the "other side of life"? If we trust in the known, can we subdue our fear of the unknown? If it's fear of death that drives a super-elderly life, perhaps we might consider something other than a prolonged life to mollify it. If we have no fear of death, perhaps we shouldn't push a prolonged life and the problems it causes.

I have long since come to respect that the soul of man transcends earthly knowledge. As Socrates asserted during his corruption trial, "[N]o one knows whether death, which men in their fear apprehend to be the greatest evil, may not be the greatest good."[139] The unyielding fact of life, i.e. death, is hardly limited to the realm of scientific knowledge or even rationality.

The meaning of death always exceeds an examination of nature and material reality. The intersections of life and death, of the known and unknown, appear nowhere so lucidly as during birth and a final disease. Who can witness these events without feeling the power of the unknown? Still, no matter how many times we approach the intersections, we still can't answer the issue that forever plagues us: what does it mean to be or not to be? That is the question.

Although science springs from human knowledge—from the Latin *scio*, to know or understand—we make sense only of portions of the universe. The universe is far too immense and abstract for any one human mind, or even all the computers in the world. As vast as the known world may be, the unknown is still vaster because it incorporates everything, including the future, the imagination, and all unrevealed science and spirituality. The King in Lewis Carroll's *Through the Looking Glass* may have had a point:

"Just look down the road and tell me if you can see either of them."

"I see nobody on the road," said Alice.

"I only wish I had such eyes to see Nobody! And at such a distance too!"

Every human—whether positivist or spiritualist—has his own point of view of the significance of life, and of death that Nobody has yet faithfully described. The debate between science and religion, however, has to begin with "man the measure"—the Somebody with a brain that acts like a clearing house of concepts. Greeks as early as Protagoras noted that "[m]an is the measure of all things, of the existence of things that are and the non-existence of things that are not."[140]

The ancient Greeks asserted that the body, providing the tools necessary for the soul, ended at death. The soul, having features unlike the body, perhaps could continue—although not with the same quality. In *Phaedo*, Socrates asks whether the soul, if it survives the death of the body, "still possesses some power and wisdom," and concludes it does retain some material attributes. Plato, however, distinguishes the body as perishable and the soul as something abstract, such as equality, beauty and the divine—and therefore is indestructible only as an immaterial quality.

A couple millennia after the ancient Greeks, Descartes, in describing dualism, agreed that the while the body follows the laws of physics, the mind, with its consciousness, doesn't.[141] "I think, therefore I am," Descartes concluded, implying that we exist because we can think.[142] Aristotle would have agreed: we exist because, from a first-person point of view, we perceive ourselves. [143] If we can think after our bodies die, our soul survives. As Plato notes, "Knowledge is nothing other than perception."[144] Our existence depends on perception and knowledge.

We watch a car speed out of sight. We know that the car's existence is likely to continue, but we don't know where. So we imagine its location. Maybe the car has gone straight down the street, or maybe someone has towed it to a junkyard and pulverized it. In the meantime, we focus on our own driving and what we ourselves perceive.

Do we really care what happened to the car? We do if we're in a similar car. As we travel down uncharted roads, we fear a dead end. Can we find a thoroughfare if we have a better GPS and intelligence and imagination? Do the unexplored roadways even exist if we can't imagine them, or if our thinking screeches to a halt as we cross a certain intersection? Einsteinian physics requires a rational material observer to detect physical existence; just as the Zen Koan of "If a tree falls in the forest, and no one is around, will it make a sound?" suggests that reality demands a material observer.

"Man the measure" assumes a single objective existence, but each new discovery, pulling us farther from our senses, pushes us into a twilight zone. And in these new unknown places, the supernatural and religion, which attribute things to forces more powerful than man's measuring sticks, already have staked their claims. Freud has used the concept of the "double" to explain man's need for an existence beyond conscious life.

> *The theme of the "double" has been very thoroughly treated … [with regard to its] connections … with reflections in mirrors, with shadows, with guardian spirits, with the belief in the soul and with the fear of death; … For the "double" was originally an insurance against the destruction of the ego, an "energetic denial of the power of death," … ; and probably the "immortal" soul was the first "double" of the body. This invention of doubling [is] a preservation against extinction …[145]*

The Safety of the Known

Science, which has tried to cast aside bias and subjectivity (at least until Einstein asserted everything was relative and every event required a movable observer), explains that souls go nowhere after death: there is no immortal soul. Nothing can think or perceive or retain knowledge after it dies. Lucretius wrote that "Death is … nothing to us, nor does it concern us one least bit, inasmuch as the nature of the mind is that of yet another mortal possession."[146] Still, science can't answer how the soul got here in the first place. (Indeed, the soul may have no meaning in science, which prefers a more measurable "psyche," "personality," or the "mind.") Science explains that death is termination, the disintegration of one level of order, the end of biological function, and the release of energy for new purpose. As such, scientific nihilism evokes an irritating spiritual rejoinder: the soul must have gone somewhere just as it came from somewhere! As students we're taught that matter and energy are convertible. Is the soul therefore material or is it spiritual energy? If it's material, as the scientists claim, why can't we pick it up and jerry-rig it back into life like Frankenstein? At conception does some abstract quality of soul, or energy component, enter the body to become material—and at death does the soul convert to energy and escape into the universe as heat?[147] Will, as Socrates believed, the energy reconstitute itself?

We can't fault scientists for trying to probe death with knowledge (or the lack of it). If the physical universe operates in the tricky language of the periodic table, mathematics and light waves, why shouldn't the genetic code, the biological blueprint for life, act as the *lingua franca* of death? Can't we decipher subtle messages about non-existence in the many types of order available to us? Or are codes just a big Rorschach test? What if God, or some other spiritual force, actually wants us to tamper with life and death by manipulating DNA? A number of writers already have suggested that God is sending explicit, if not weird messages, in DNA.[148] Can God and man at least speak a common language when confronting the unknown?

"Mathematics is the language with which God has written the universe," says Galileo. Even if the spiritual universe remains a mystery to our senses, we certainly have the intellectual ability to explore large chunks of the material universe. Given our physical limitations, however, we can observe death only from the platform of a living human. If we try to order our soul with mathematics, we never succeed—we look like tailors dressing thin air. Some abstractions push us to conjure up enduring objects, like an idol or an icon. In our attempt to understand death, we objectify it as an angel, or a mummy or the Grim Reaper. Ironically, we give life to death—we objectify the subjective and give it purpose.

Obviously we can't survey the unknown—especially death—*only* using measuring sticks. While positivists might say that life is X years long and has Y measurable components like a heartbeat or brainwaves, X times Y no more gauges the full meaning of death than a blackboard full of equations transforms itself into art. On the one hand, death is like a limit in calculus. On the other hand, death is like an infinite imaginary number in a galactic black hole. Death is elusive and filled with a billion possibilities that confound even the Einsteins. Could it be that life, death, nature and God remain tied to nothing more than a human puzzle that combats the emptiness of space? Why do we, as living humans, even impose such riddles on ourselves?

The Abstract

Because man's first rational thoughts caused him to ponder the purpose and beauty of the sun, stars, and sky, and even himself, his limited knowledge pushed him to connect to—and rebel against—things greater and more subtle than himself. Beauty intrigued man long before he could define it with neurons in the brain. Jung argues that man's emergence from nature, and his recognition of "problems," began only with his acquisition of knowledge.[149] Knowledge gave man the ability to challenge the long-settled judgments of nature.

Religion treats man's knowledge ambiguously—both as a danger and as a jumping off point to the truth and meaning of death. Western religion often equates knowledge with original sin, the moving away from nature, the expulsion from paradise. Still, religion also recognizes life as the known and death as something abstract and spiritual and never truly known.[150] The Bible asserts that God's knowledge, rather than the knowledge of man, provides the ultimate meaning of life and death: "As unknown, and yet well known; as dying, and, behold, we live; as chastened, and not killed."[151] Eastern and western religions promise an afterlife if the soul achieves the right kind of knowledge during life.

No matter how man approaches existence—whether through science or spirituality—reconciling the material and abstract universes remains as perplexing as unifying the body and the soul. One portion of "enlightened" mankind attributes the essence of meaning to the laws of nature in which knowledge and perception predominate; the other "enlightened" portion credits it to spiritual forces—and so each tries to fit a bad shoe on the foot of the other. Love, happiness, nirvana—ideas that dwell in abstraction—rely on the spiritual power of the mind.

Spinoza argues that regardless of reality or abstraction, the mind, body and universe are all one reality—that nature and God are the same.[152] Any genuine understanding of the universe and ourselves, at least while we're alive, has to begin with an objective construction of reality. As Aristotle asserts, "To say of what is that it is not, or of what is not that it is, is false; while to say of what is that it is, and of what is not that it is not, is true" [153] Although we are born with certain instincts—*a priori* knowledge, as Kant would say—we lack the inherent ability "to know" much beyond the information brought through our senses. We rely on learned logic to correct our senses, to order the information, to determine "what [really] is," and to satisfy our curiosity.

In short, we can look only into non-science and speculation to complete the answers to the deeper non-measurable questions about life and death. Because death belongs to a world we can't experience (with our five senses anyway), we have just our imaginations to guide us. Perception doesn't help us at all. Socrates asserted that the fear of death—professing to know the unknown—is a pretense of wisdom.[154] Nevertheless, something has imbued our life force with an unquenchable curiosity to seek purpose and meaning, and to answer the questions no matter how confounding.

Knowledge as Direction

Jung writes that the "[e]xpansion of life, usefulness, efficiency, the cutting of a figure in social life, the shrewd steering of offspring into suitable marriages and good positions—are not these purpose enough? Unfortunately this is not enough meaning or purpose for many persons who see in the approach of old age a mere diminution of life, and who look upon their earlier ideals only as something faded and worn out. ... It is particularly fatal for such people to look backward. For them a prospect and a goal in the future are indispensable. This is why all great religions hold the promise of a life beyond; it makes it possible for mortal man to live the second half of life with as much perseverance and aim as the first. For the man of today the enlargement of life and its culmination are plausible goals; but the idea of life after death seems to him questionable or beyond belief."[155]

Certainly we can simplify the connection between our personal limits and meaning by recalling that direction takes place only with a reference. Everything is relative, as Einstein again might say. Give someone a map coordinate and he'll orient himself. Take it away and a person becomes a random particle drawn to the most alluring force. Limits produce coordinates; and death, the ultimate limit, establishes direction to life. "I built an empire at age 40!" or "I suffered three strokes before I reached 50 years." Without death, Sartre wrote, there can be no life.[156] At the least, perhaps with some expandable non-frightening barrier, our appreciation of progress will continue.

Without any limits we will become aimless, and the common refrain easily might become, "Where am I, and where am I going in my life?"

If time and aging disappear, can we substitute money, fame, or experience as equal coordinates? Some will say that, of course, life has value without a termination—because life already offers a billion markers other than death. We don't travel alone through space: we remain connected to the earth, to nature, to other humans and animals. As humanists point out, we easily find meaning in ethnicity, status, family or achievements—rather than limited time. "I am the foremost Aleut fisherman!" or "I love my family." Even if death never forms a demarcation with life, we don't have to feel purposeless or that life has no meaning without death, or feel existential dread. Like dumping fear for courage, we will reorient ourselves. Besides, most of us today rarely refer to our own deaths, or even to any substantive reason we're here. We spend our days taking drugs, eating fast food, thinking about work or family or why George W. Bush is who he is. Short term meaning already replaces long term meaning. Short term meaning may numb us to the universe, but it erases our fear.

Adding to knowledge is like an antidepressant—it boosts us, gives us a temporary way out, restores a feeling of power and freedom as we approach death, intensifies the meaning we may lose with immortality. The unknown, or ignorance, brings forward death in that it projects foreboding, pain, confusion and misdirection. As Anna Quindlen writes, "A closed mind is a catafalque."[157] In a poem called the *Puppet,* the author writes, "To the old I would teach that death comes not with old age but with forgetting."[158] So, if existentialists fear that the end of death will spell the end of meaning, we might consider knowledge itself as a substitute for life, and the unknown, and our ignorance of it, as a substitute for death.

But by focusing only on science, aren't we simply trying to whitewash our fear of an inexorable death? Isn't the dilemma of science the understanding that no matter how powerful it becomes, no matter what anesthetic it injects into us, it can't save our mortal souls forever? No one therefore should underestimate the marker of religion in providing man a *raison d'etre*—both the spiritual power of the unseen and the hard organizational structure of the churches. Whether religion will survive in the face of human immortality can be answered simply: it will. Regardless of the power of the brain, spiritualism, the unmeasuring probe into the unknown, will never become the weak sister in the search for meaning. Even if science kills death, spiritualists won't give up their hold over the unknown. Each new discovery of life will reveal an unknown piece of death.

Despite what my high school teacher insisted, science struggles to deal with the known, while religion remains far more comfortable with the unknown. The unknown always will outweigh the known no matter how progressive humans become. By definition, we will never know everything we don't know.[159]

In this tension, barriers will continue to arise: first in perceiving and doing the right things while we're alive, and secondly when science fails to numb us with the fact that we won't live forever. We have seen throughout history that as western science offends spiritual doctrine, theology reacts. We see this dynamic in the middle-east where western civilization, filled with gadgets and toys, often offends Islamic cultures. The push of one causes the push-back of the other. Of course, we can expect conflict at the barrier between the positivists who will advocate human solutions and theologians who will defend the universe as it is and always will be.

Strangely, the conflict itself supplies meaning and purpose. Conflict implies boundaries and positions and, therefore, the coordinates for further steering. We may eliminate death, but we never will eliminate the unknown— or the conflict between science and religion, which is, after all, the conflict between the known and unknown.

CHAPTER X

The Irreconcilability of Killing

Word over all, beautiful as the sky,
Beautiful that war and all its deeds of carnage must in
time be utterly lost,
That the hands of the sisters Death and Night incessantly
softly wash again,
and ever again, this soil'd world;
For my enemy is dead, a man divine as myself is dead,
I look where he lies white-faced and still in the coffin—I
draw near,
Bend down and touch lightly with my lips the white face
in the coffin.

— Walt Whitman, *Reconciliation*

Death is ugly and cruel. Whether a person dies peacefully or violently, few can witness it without profound emotions. The mass of bodies lying in the streets of Haiti in January 2010 became more than we could comprehend. With the quantity and quality of death continually numbing us, the video of an innocent young woman, Neda Agha-Soltan, randomly shot by a government sniper in Tehran in June 2009, still shocked and angered us all. We continually witness not only the unjust killing of humans, but the loss of human potential for no apparent purpose.

As we try to preserve moral freedom and curtail natural death, perhaps we should consider how ruthlessly new forces fight back. Novel diseases or Malthusian conditions always seem to find ways to kill weak and strong humans alike. If, as we've already seen, retroviruses employ clever and elusive ways to alter the human genome,[160] we might predict that death will mutate in creative ways to thwart eternal life. Will super-agers themselves generate some personality idiosyncrasy and kill themselves? Will future generations, angry at the economic burdens eclipsing even multi-trillion dollar stimulus plans, seek out and lynch centenarians?[161] Will abortions gain public favor to reduce pressure on resources? Will society itself change course and advocate suicide as a way of making room for others?

The questions compel us again—this time from a moral point of view—to consider whether death is not only a dynamic organism, but a "just" organism that exerts itself as forcefully and relentlessly as life. Death won't quit even if people last a thousand years—and particularly if its own survival is at stake. Why shouldn't we expect more potent forms of death when humans drive too hard for immortality?

The irony is truly amazing. While we try to deny the power of death, death tries to deny our power. We set out a game of chess, and death switches the game to whack-a-mole. Death obliges us to accept rules we never knew: it creates new strains of antibiotic-resistant bacteria; it creates unimagined disaster during the reentry of a space shuttle; it fries people in Ukraine with nuclear power plants. What nineteenth century human could conceive of these new forms of death? What new form awaits us when the mole pops up again?

It's not as if death won't cooperate. We promote its viciousness during conflict. As General George Patton commented during World War II, "No bastard ever won a war by dying for his country. He won it by making the other poor dumb bastard die for his country."[162] Every army on earth searches for brutal ways to inflict death: napalm, anthrax, nuclear annihilation, to name a few. With larger populations and disputes, we can expect ever more pitiless ways to kill. Can we therefore really expect death to do piece work for just us?

Walt Whitman, who served in a field hospital during the Civil War, saw death in his 1865 poem *Reconciliation* not only as an immoral and horrible thing, but as a purifier. But even if death does our cleansing in times of war, St. Matthew has warned us to respect the commandment against murder. "Love your enemies, bless them that curse you, do good to them that hate you."[163] The great dilemma occurs in squaring how not to kill our enemies while surviving long lives. No decent human should love a Hitler or Stalin, but if we refuse to kill them or anyone who perpetrates evil, how do we preserve freedom, justice and long life for ourselves and those we love? Does cruelty beget cruelty even if "our" cruelty is just and moral? Does kindness toward an evil enemy really beget kindness—or our extinction?

The manner and "justice" of terminating life begs the definition of justice. John Stuart Mill wrote that "It is universally considered just that each person should obtain that (whether good or evil) which he deserves; and unjust that he should obtain a good, or be made to undergo an evil which he does not deserve."[164] If so, as Mills asserts, then a Lincoln or a Mother Theresa deserves a long life, but an evil person deserves death as soon as possible. Within the huge in-between, what qualities deserve any consideration at all? Indeed, do we have a moral *obligation* to save a life or reward anyone with a long life?

The considerations may rest on the framework. A utopian society, full of perfect justice, may produce perfectly deserving people; but one that rewards only pious behavior may imply that a religious terrorist deserves a long life. A society that rewards survival of the physically fittest over all else may imply that a health-conscious psychopath deserves a long life. Within the context of our present market oriented civilization, in which we expect consideration for consideration, perhaps a super-long life requires a super-big contribution to society. Because society is diverse, many good deeds justify the costs of extending a life. On the other hand, rampant self-indulgence probably doesn't.

If someone harms society, whether intentionally or not, why should society tolerate him at all? Still, as in the case of capital punishment, it's one thing to let a harmful person live out a natural life in prison; it's another to kill him. Nevertheless, despite the violence and callousness, a moral civilization appreciates that killing a tyrant is sometimes necessary—like destroying a dangerous cancerous cell. Many writers have concluded that well-meaning pacifism—turning your cheek to evil because any killing is odious—allowed Hitler to conduct his murderous acts on millions who themselves deserved much longer lives. Not ironically, Hitler himself saw pacifism as weakness and a corruption of survival of the fittest. In his book *Totalitarianism*, Michael Curtis writes that "For Hitler pacifism paralyzed 'the natural strength of the self-preservation of people.' ... Life was a cruel struggle and had no object but the preservation of the species."

As early as the fourth century, in *Civitas Dei,* St. Augustine proposed the concept of the "just war." In response to the barbarian invasions, Augustine balanced Matthew's pacifism with Roman admonitions to vanquish your enemies before they vanquish you. According to Augustine, the "real evils in war were not war itself but the love of violence and cruelty, greed and the ... lust for rule that so often accompanied it."[165] Augustine proposed conditions for a just war: proper authority, proper cause, a reasonable chance of success, and the protection of civilians from harm. In other words, it's sometimes okay for pacifists to terminate evil, provided the means aren't too drastic.

It always has been easier to kill than preserve: killing merely requires a cathartic release; preserving takes time and effort. Great civilizations nevertheless prefer to save life rather than destroy it, but they equivocate. Each year the U.S. spends approximately two trillion dollars publicly and privately on life-preserving activities (including healthcare, Medicare, social security, food and nutrition and disability insurance), while the rest of the world spends half that amount combined.[166] Civilized society also licenses death by those in uniform and promotes a broad industry to assist. During the Bush years, the United States allocated something like a trillion dollars per year for possible war (including off-budget items for Iraq and the war on terror).[167] The rest of the world combined, including Russia, China, Iran and North Korea, budgeted only somewhat more than half a trillion dollars.[168]

The interesting aspect isn't that the U.S. outspent everyone else (which was true in almost everything), but that humans throughout the world, in a fairly constant ratio, effectively take two steps forward to save themselves and one step backward to kill themselves. (Curiously, cancer researchers have hypothesized similar energy ratios affecting cancer and apoptosis.[169]) Social killing, or planning for death, also is far less accidental than we think. If we include all the effort devoted to end-of-life care, funerals and estates, it's clear that death occupies a huge percentage of the time and resources of any society (and any complex organism).

Our social efforts to manage life and death seem schizophrenic. On the one hand, we try to grant ourselves immortality, and on the other hand, we try to limit our numbers. It simply may be that the life force requires more energy than the death force. Or it may be that our collective subconscious steers us through our actions. (Jung certainly thought so.[170]) By directing death to the weakest segments of our population, we innately may be preserving the toughest segments and thereby strengthening our society. Hitler had his insane ideas about the strongest: physical, blonde, Aryan, German. The "strongest," however, depend on the communities in which they spawn and live. Perhaps muscle-headed blondes excelled in Nazi Germany, but in a modern technological society, bigger brains probably do better.

Life and death therefore seem to impose their own moral imperative: manage life and death in some form for the survival of the best and brightest. Will this group include the super-elderly? Kant and others have argued that deontological ethics, or the ethics of duty, "require" us "freely" to base our moral choices on good acts and not worry about the consequences: good means theoretically justify any end. Teleological ethics, on the other hand, require us to consider the consequences: moral ends sometimes do justify harsh means in order for the species to survive. Deontology forbids bad intentions; teleological ethics grants the moral authority, if necessary, to kill one to save a hundred others.

Some, of course, will dispute that the *duty* of individuals to exercise this sort of moral freedom over collective life and death is moral at all—but rather is an amoral determinism bound up only in instinct. David Hume was convinced that humans possessed inherent moral sense that needed no conscious reasoning. He wrote that "Since reason alone can never produce any action or give rise to volition, I infer, that the same faculty is as incapable of preventing volition, or of disputing the preference with any passion or emotion. … Reason is, and ought only to be the slave of the passions, and can never pretend to any other office than to serve and obey them."[171] Writers have interpreted Hume to assert that moral sense is instinctual, and that moral reasoning, good or bad, is simply an emergent outgrowth.[172] If so, it means that society pays attention only to the passions of the mob.

However, reason does motivate, and morality requires conscious choice. Inanimate objects may exhibit behavior that mimics morality, but it's not the same thing. Morality requires far more than raw random freedom. It requires consciousness and the ability to understand dilemmas and to influence a result. Scientists who once viewed the universe as completely mechanistic, recognize that individual freedom, even if not "reasonable," exists at all levels of organization and plays as much a part of the universal fabric as law and order. When we examine quantum mechanics, we expect "uncertainty" as part of a more deterministic overarching system.[173] As in the case of genetic switching, cellular function doesn't always conform to predictable order—to conform without deviation not only disrupts the "independent judgment" of some cells, but hinders species evolution, which may use epigenetic (or non-genetic) factors, as well as variation, for selection.[174] Individual humans exert at least as much freedom as individual electrons and cells, but coupled with human consciousness, they can and do push a matter in one direction or another that is anything but random.

Of course, at an individual level, we never know exactly what free will and reason will do. An individual invents a life-saving machine or blows himself up in a restaurant. Sociologists and politicians have their own views of moral freedom, reason and determinism, and adapt them to their frameworks. American John Gardner, for example, mixing and yet distilling the concepts, asserts that "Freedom and responsibility, liberty and duty: that's the deal."[175] Here in America, if we want political freedom, we assume moral obligations: we make use of our freedom to create a fair and just order.

Even the most moral people can mold reason to their particular sense of right and wrong. *The Washington Post* published an article in November 2007 about an Israeli doctor who saves Palestinian children by day and, as an Israeli helicopter pilot, fires rockets into Palestinian terrorists by night. "After decades of war," Laura Blumenfeld wrote, "what might be madness in another society passes for normal in Israel. … In the Bible, Ecclesiastes declares: 'There is … a time to kill, and a time to heal.' Yuval [the doctor-pilot] is doing both, at the same time."[176]

Debates rarely include discussion, much less advocacy, of moral killing, or of less drastic means of eliminating people by simply evicting them from an overburdened society. It all reminds us again of corrupt frameworks, of Hitler, of his *Lebensraum,* of his flagrant claims that one group of humans has the right to take away life and living space from another. Perfect utopias in which we live peacefully may come at a high price—the exact opposite of Gardner's deal: the elimination of both individual freedom and moral duty. In a completely rational world devoid of randomness, instinct and subtlety, but filled with predictability and fiats, we won't ponder where the elderly have gone or why we have adequate living space. We will maximize a good life and minimize a bad death.

If we look honestly at our positions—and our budgetary expenditures—we see that we already are partners with death. If we assume a moral responsibility for imposing death, we must balance the responsibility with life and freedom and moderation. Totalitarian societies give us a glimpse of what can go wrong: we will kill more often, more openly, and more precisely. The freedom and liberty inherent in Gardner's "deal" easily could mutate into an unjust and grotesque responsibility, and wholesale slaughter aimed at the most vulnerable, in order to protect against overpopulation.[177]

Humanity can't become so humane that it becomes inhumane. There are always limits we can't reconcile with our desire for immortality. We must recognize that death is cunning and will remain with us forever—even as we alter genes and cure disease to deprive it of its power. To the extent that we can control some natural forces, we still must measure our actions to do the least harm, even if we have to tolerate some death to achieve it.

CHAPTER XI

No Geezer Left Behind

As history so often demonstrates, powers gained for one
purpose are often used for other, less noble ones. We are
about to harness powers over our own (human) nature ...
for our own well-intentioned purposes. But the knowledge
that provides this power does not teach us how to use it.
And given our fallibility, that should give us pause. ...
There may be occasions in life when the only means
available for achieving a desired end is a means that ...
would be wrong to employ. ... When we refuse to achieve
a good outcome by doing ... wrong ... we are not guilty of
causing ... suffering. ... If our duty to prevent [existing]
harm and suffering were always overriding ... we could
not live nobly and justly.

— The President's Council on Bioethics

How will society change if super-aging takes hold? Clearly it will evolve with its members.

Life, as everyone knows, isn't fair, equal, or even very democratic. Life probably won't become fairer if everyone takes a lion's share of it. But if the right to immortality ever comes up for a vote, who wouldn't favor it? Most would argue that immortality improves life. Some would vote against the idea, of course, arguing that the conditions surrounding immortality not only upset the balances of nature and weaken the population, but make life worse in general. Heated debates already have arisen regarding rationing and the benefits and risks of biotechnology.[178] Positivists like de Grey advocate the "equal rights" that a long life supposedly affords, while naturalists fear the loss of muscle with non-competitive selection. Theologians and moralists worry about the right and wrong of the entire process. No doubt, super-aging will curtail the individuality and freedom we already have, and very well could promote a peculiar brand of centralized social order.

As we've discussed, aging beyond the grandmother period depends on human intervention—again, much like maintaining a car. Everyone knows that cars fall apart because entropy butts heads even with plastic bumpers. Maintenance plans usually presume that we want to take care of our cars for at least 100,000 miles and that shops will help us if we can't—and who can anymore? Manufacturers can provide only so much built-in maintenance. (Navigation devices require downloads of data, and computerized engine warnings insist on attention.) In the U.S., the free market generally distributes maintenance shops: the more cars, the more locations. But governments increasingly control maintenance because a dangerous car harms more than one driver. Many states impose mandatory inspections, while others just let cars fall apart on the roads.

If someday government makes us maintain cars for 300,000 miles, it no doubt will mandate minimum body maintenance for 300 years. Health will become the largest industry on the planet and super-aging will revolutionize it. Clinics, gyms and health stores will pop up like genetically modified corn. Imagine a one stop body lube: next door someone works on our aging cars as we walk into a quick-clinic for a thirty minute MRI, protein check, and blood transfusion complete with necessary drugs. In some parts store down the street, mechanics will be growing or constructing spare eyes, knees, and livers for broken bodies.[179] For both cars and people, servicers will match our wallet. With enough money, we can drink vitamin-laced mint juleps for the next millennium.

But without money, or adequate insurance, we as super-agers can expect to find ourselves floating in a big human pool without a life vest. Only if our government enacts a bill called "No Geezer Left Behind," will we remain super-elderly (and super-happy) very long. If government responds at all to our demands for indefinitely long life support, it will address them through agencies, committees and bureaucracies. As a certainty it will mandate universal physical fitness and preventive treatment to keep costs down. It will shove us through tests like pills in a sorting bin. As a result, we won't experience larger doses of *joie de vivre*, but rather enormous pressure as hordes of fellow geezers do push-ups and enzyme checks together. Compulsory inspections and governmental intervention in every aspect of our health will become the norm. We can forget about smoking or eating those chocolate donuts we like.

Because our dependence on government will make us wards of the state, almost like pets, our political rights will atrophy with our muscles. Bio-scientists, bio-positivists and bio-naturalists necessarily will dominate, and they will become paternalistic, saving us like whales. We hope that our kids, or great great grand kids, won't abandon us or grant experts *carte blanche* authority to determine our fate. As the town-hall reactions to publicly administered healthcare showed in August 2009, we Americans have a temper and don't like a government of elites—even if they mean well and are right. We fear expert fiats. The 2002 report of the *President's Council on Bioethics*, addressing cloning, evidenced a distrust of bio-scientists as deep as the distrust of Wall Street types who nearly destroyed our economy six years later.

Not surprisingly, the bioethics council took a moral position contrary to de Grey's right to live forever.[180] No individual has the right, the council implied, to live better, or forever, if science causes harm along the way. Genetic engineering is so rife with risk to even a few that it has neither a duty nor a right to stamp out suffering to the masses with its use.[181] Implied in the report is that both deontological and teleological ethics are forbidden: there is no right to do harm, whether intentionally or unintentionally. An individual can't experiment if there is any chance of harm to others—or, it appears, even to himself.

Obviously humans can't eliminate harm any more than they can eliminate risk. Risk of harm simply depends on where humans place it, intentionally or accidentally. All evolution, including political evolution, depends on environment. Francis Fukuyama, who served on the bioethics council, has written a number of influential books that examine the evolution of technology. In *Our Posthuman Future: Consequences of the Biotechnology Revolution,* Fukuyama allows that science can go too far in some environments. He fears that "bio's" (my term), by overstepping moral freedom, may turn society into a "giant nursing home." Further, he worries that human dignity will suffer if bios alter human nature.

Both bio-moralists and bio-positivists may be preparing for battle. The bioethics council's no-risk position on research, however, is a stretch. Life always has been full of peril, both in means and ends. Nature respects the freedom and risk in evolution. Obviously, science shouldn't fillet reasonable moral concerns, but it also shouldn't have to overcome every risk, especially if the potential result saves humanity.

Medicine generally strikes a reasonable balance. While it stalks innovation to battle death and debilitation, good doctors exert moral restraint when they weigh the dangers of new treatments. Should a doctor prescribe a drug to reduce painful arthritis if it means increasing the possibility of a heart attack? Should a doctor save one Siamese twin if it kills the other? The Hippocratic Oath demands that doctors choose life without long-term concerns:

> *I will follow that system of regimen ... for the benefit of*
> *my patients, and abstain from whatever is deleterious and*
> *mischievous. I will give no deadly medicine to anyone if asked,*
> *nor suggest any such counsel; and in like manner I will not give*
> *to a woman a pessary to produce abortion.*

But perhaps the Hippocratic Oath is too one-sided. Considering that natural death is still a regulator of a healthy body and population, too much artificial intervention to keep the super-elderly alive may result in a decline in overall health: the more chronically sick people survive, the worse average health becomes. The moral implications of extraordinary human intervention may shock us: more harm to the population may occur in saving lives than by permitting natural death.

As we have discussed and bio-moralists might argue, if we tamper too much with mortality, death may transform itself. At the cellular level, it may favor mutations that prevent pregnancy or increase the percentage of defective births,[182] cause telomeres to shorten rather than lengthen, halt apoptosis to promote new forms of cancer, or advance new forms of drug resistant bacteria and viruses. At a bodily level, we may expect more mental illness, homicides, suicides, abortions and pleasure risk-taking. At the social level, death may trigger national wars over resources, or limit food, deplete minerals, and encourage aggressive dictators who have no hesitation to commit genocides. In short, there are many ways for death to wreck an artificial system.

Even if super-aging alone lacks the power to create or destroy society, it can push society into directions that trigger new responses. Stephen Jay Gould and Niles Eldredge use the term *punctuated equilibrium* (with roots in Thomas Kuhn's "paradigm shift") to describe the rapid, rather than gradual adjustments that occur with drastic environmental changes. To be sure, when enough events overwhelm a system, a revolution will occur. In the case of an overload of super-geezers, the strain may trigger such a shift.

Paradigm shifts are rarely monolithic—and smaller parts of a larger system nearly always advance at different rates and with different purpose. Ernst Mayr, who influenced Gould and Eldredge, first recognized that internal organs of bodies evolve at different rates. A kidney or heart of a human remains similar to a pig's, while the brain has moved on in size and function. This principle of "mosaic evolution" applies to society: urban architecture may change rapidly while the roads that entangle it grow more slowly. Super-aging humans can become a social cluster that changes slower than economic and political parts. The super-elderly could become a vestigial appendix of some social behemoth, ready for excision if the behemoth becomes ill.

Certainly new physical and social traits will develop if the super-elderly clog the pipes of a complex evolutionary system. Our size, for example, may decrease if food resources fail with an expanding population.[183] Social altruism may decline: business moguls may regress into pre-Hobbesian clans and focus resources only on themselves. Post-Hobbesian technicians, perhaps having more brains than brawn, may invent super-tools to protect only themselves from a tsunami of wheelchairs.

Notwithstanding ossification of one segment of society, an evolving social framework will try to avoid complete collapse.[184] Even if super-geezers retain their health as they age and somehow hog control of society without killing it, something novel always will challenge their authority. Max Planck wrote that "[a] new scientific truth does not triumph by convincing its opponents and making them see the light, but rather because its opponents eventually die, and a new generation grows up that is familiar with it."[185] Super-agers therefore will merely appear vested in social control—because any change in favor of social survival, however minute, will erode their power.

Younger people will grow tired of preserving their great great grandparents, especially if events demand rapid change. Indeed, a dynamic social order can never emerge quietly from a society stuck in park. While innovation often does materialize out of the most frustrating situations, there is no guarantee that a stronger society will evolve peacefully. As people age, they often lose the strength or relevant skills to work, let alone lead others. An obsolete segment of the economy, neither functioning nor relaxing, therefore may be left defenseless to wither away as others ignore it or take more drastic action for survival.

In an extreme situation, society could fold altogether. As Jared Diamond writes, poor environmental and social relationships remain major markers of destroyed societies, but society's *responses* to its problems remain even more significant. The natural response to survival threats usually involves adaptation and competition. The whole purpose of adaptation and any competition, whether for profit or survival, is to win. And winning implies inequality. If the super-elderly have to compete on a level playing field for limited resources, they will lose.

Economic waves lap at old-age protectionism, dated ideas and products. Even if persistence keeps our old '57 Chevy running, most consumers favor a new Porsche or a sleek new green machine that gets a hundred miles to the gallon. In fact, technology, economy and evolution always prefer efficient and youthful packages—just as society and the natural life-and-death system do. The character Gordon Gekko asserts trenchantly in the movie *Wall Street* that greed and fear motivate capitalism. Greed and fear also motivate survival.

If this sounds like evolution's Red Queen theory (taken from Lewis Carroll's *Through the Looking Glass*), it's because the life-and-death system makes everyone run faster and faster to stay even. Unfortunately, no one, even a marathoner, has the stamina to sprint forever in life's Olympics.[186] The elderly, once upon a time permitted to drop out of the race, will face a peculiar dilemma: if they become too sedentary they are doomed; if they want to do better than a nursing home, they must remain driven. It's yet more evidence of the Devil's Bargain in which a person can have a good life, or a long life, but not both.

What all of this suggests, of course, is that like a bad genetic code that leaves a species weak, and requires outside protection, a non-competitive society requires central planning to enforce equality and to avoid rocking an unbalanced and overloaded boat. If a society filled with static immortals relies only on democracy and the free market for its survival, we can expect harsh dog-eat-dog conduct. People may live long lives, but they may have very little if they produce very little. An extended life may require an extended productive period and brutal competition with younger, more powerful individuals. There may be no rest for the weary.

Although markets may have no social concern for the super-elderly who lack power, business depends on government as a regulator, and government no doubt will force business to show some concern—especially if society demands extended life in the first place. But governments can never require private business to respond to every demand. Government therefore will have a choice: either to support a social equality (but economic inequality) that rewards super-aging tortoises and punishes younger rabbits, or to let the market function, leaving creaky geezers vulnerable to oblivion.

Perhaps a strong political system will strike a peaceful equilibrium. Perhaps government will protect both those who contribute and those who no longer can. Perhaps government will stray from liberal democracy, or even a republic, toward an authoritarian form, applicable to some, but not all, based on age or wealth. In all events, a government forced to address a large super-aging population will differ radically from what we have today. We may not like it.

CHAPTER XII

Messing With Mother Nature

Because I could not stop for Death –
He kindly stopped for me –
The Carriage held but just Ourselves –
And Immortality.

— Emily Dickinson

We need powerful soldiers to confront the pale horseman of the apocalypse. If the decisions regarding death shift completely away from nature and toward society, we may find ourselves using the extreme tools of the state to counter population imbalance and the misery it brings. Not only may the state provide authoritarian safety to enhance resources and preserve life, but it may employ violence to cull the herd. Any organized governmental action may expose yet another dangerous Faustian conceit: that technology can forge social weapons and command any threat out of existence.

Can we substitute our knowledge—our judgment—for Mother Nature's and God's? Certainly we have to try to balance life and death without radical social behavior. Pushed by markets and a hyper-demanding population, we can work hard at adjusting conditions for the good of all humanity. Still, we seem to work twice as hard to extend lives as to end them. We already recruit DNA to attack pestilence and famine. Molecular marauders confront viruses and bacteria; disease becomes less of an acute curse and more of a nuisance. We assign ourselves the tedious minute-to-minute tasks of adjusting life and death to individual situations—from forcing medicines at precise times to monitoring a world of heart rates and kidney function, to controlling sexual preferences and criminal activities. Someday soon nano-soldiers may put an end to AIDS, multiple sclerosis, and the afflictions of Lou Gehrig and Parkinson. We may devise genetic tricks to grow ever more food and conquer starvation. We may become an even more powerful, pervasive and persistent presence as our scientists find newer ways to leap over natural impediments in a single bound.

Unfortunately, we may have become crusaders of life without enough thought of the consequences. As regulators, we can't match nature in its ability to balance life and death. We can't count on volcanic eruptions and floods, or dictators, to dampen population—nor should we. We have to find humane ways to control population.

Unlike us, Mother Nature generally operates with little drama. We don't see the enormous number of biological conflicts she mediates every second. Her physiology cues our conduct. When we become thirsty, we drink. When we run, our heart rate jumps and our breathing quickens. Although her regulators normally operate our bodies quietly, they pump adrenalin into our hearts to shove us out of the way of runaway cars and they compel us to eat worms when we're starving. But nature sometimes turns cruel by unleashing diseases and disasters. It only takes a Haitian or Chilean earthquake for us to realize our limited power and nature's capricious justice. In times of acute crisis, we see how far ahead of man Mother Nature is—and how forcefully she regulates.

If we really intend to replace nature, we face more work than bringing two strands of human DNA together or enforcing term limits with a few bullets. Beginning and ending life requires the blending of billions of micro and macro events. Life and death has to work not just in the summer of life, when the living is easy, but in winter, when the living isn't so easy. Any humane regulator in the system also must balance mercy for the sick with bolstering the healthy.

Our social machines will have to mobilize and monitor billions of people from birth to death. A baby with a bar code will have to join a community. If too few babies roll off the assembly line, we will have to terminate some old-model humans or speed production of new models to support society. Or (as in Germany) we may have to redesign society itself to protect the young as producers and reproducers, and not as canon fodder. If we oversupply the world with babies, we may have to park them somewhere, or recycle them, or else we may run out of resources (as in parts of India and China).

Perhaps, before we put ourselves into this strange situation, we should reconsider the genius of the existing natural system. In general, societies, like their economies, react as much to invisible forces as visible ones. Nature already pays attention to mobility and reproduction rates. After "natural" wars and disasters, for example, most populations return to some sort of equilibrium—even if the equilibrium hints of new frameworks.[187] Sometimes society, however, using technologies nature never anticipated, radically upsets the balances. China's "one child policy" has reduced its population growth and appears to have saved itself from the drastic consequences of overpopulation. But as revealed by the Sichuan earthquake of 2007—which left many parents without children, and many children without parents—China routinely faces policy problems when disasters strike.[188] And recently, policy makers have discovered that the shortage of children is slowing growth, impairing China's support to its accumulating elderly, and forcing it to reconsider its policy altogether.[189] The new man-made equilibrium also suggests more tectonic shifts in the future.

We can't ignore that humans share a common purpose with nature in wanting to survive. Although man, with his acquired knowledge, constantly bickers with Mother Nature, he also seeks familial cooperation and common purpose. As emotion motivates a human to satisfy unconscious desires, or as the need for resources drives war, survival motivates the entire life-and-death system to choose the "right" direction. We have much in common with nature.

Who other than Arnold Schwarzenegger, the *governator* (nee *terminator*), qualifies as the best regulator of a humane life-and-death machine? Should he imitate Mother Nature in the form of a man-made chemical compound that pervades every cell, or an almighty spirit floating in the heavens? How about a mega-computer? Certainly genes already possess the proven skill to run the machine. Not only do they monitor every one of the 100 trillion cells in the body, they carry out complex instructions for each of them. Genes have no moral problem flipping switches and killing themselves or others for the greater survival.

Dawkins theorizes in *The Selfish Gene* that the viewpoint of the gene, if it really has one, provides the best understanding of the qualifications of a regulator.[190] Selfishness and altruism, or survival and sacrifice, are really two sides of the same coin feeding the machines—perhaps, as some suggest, because species survival favors greater mathematical replication of genes.[191] Selection always begins at the genetic level. We suspect that cells, bodies, species and populations really do answer to genes. Therefore, why not let our DNA control it all from the bottom of the heap rather than from Washington?

Science, with its tinkering, already has altered nature's life-and-death relationship with us. If science truly intends to dominate the natural world, however, we had better understand the implications of human tampering. With six billion people running around, life-and-death is a giant binary system with more combinations than even science can calculate. We will need lots of computers and even more wisdom in order to reach a balance that doesn't rest on an active fault line.

Chapter XIII

Seven Moral Challenges

*The reader will easily believe, that from what I had heard and
seen, my keen appetite for perpetuity of life was much abated.
I grew heartily ashamed of the pleasing visions I had formed;
and thought no tyrant could invent a death into which I
would not run with pleasure, from such a life. ... [I wish]
I could send a couple of [immortal] Struldbrugs to my own
country, to arm our people against the fear of death; but this, it
seems, is forbidden by the fundamental laws of the kingdom ...
I could not but agree, that the laws of this kingdom relative
to the Struldbrugs were founded upon the strongest reasons,
and such as any other country would be under the necessity of
enacting, in the like circumstances. Otherwise, as avarice is
the necessary consequence of old age, those immortals would in
time become proprietors of the whole nation, and engross the
civil power, which, for want of abilities to manage, must end
in the ruin of the public.*

— Jonathan Swift, *Gulliver's Travels*

The huge wrench that mass immortality throws into the machinery of life
will lead to more than a few moral dilemmas. But even the smaller wrench
of improved longevity will do the same. As Edward Lorenz suggested, the
flapping of a butterfly's wings in Florida could affect a typhoon in Bali.[192] A
new order will emerge, but will it unleash the evils of Pandora?

First Challenge:
Mother Nature and God May Deepen the Split From Science

Despite their good intentions, positivists sometimes come dangerously close
to resurrecting Nazi and communist practices. Positivists like de Grey see

nothing wrong, and virtually all good, with prolonging an already long life—even at the price of extreme social control and loss of freedom. Such extremism isn't limited to positivists, however. Militant naturalists see human culture wrecking the precarious balances of nature. As in their opposition to hunting, forest firefighting, or the carbon levels in the atmosphere, some naturalists violently dispute the human right to interfere with any natural events. Radical religionists often share the same disdain to a society without a soul.

During any period of drastic changes, tensions rocket between advocates of various sides. Social writers and theorists long have expected splits between man-centered cultures and those resting on spirit and nature. In the seventeenth century, Hobbes in *Leviathan* recognized it.[193] Two centuries later, Comte described the tension in the emergence of positivism from religion and naturalism. In 1939, in *Civilization and its Discontents*, Freud lamented the permanent dissatisfaction existing between a rigid society afraid of disorder and death, and risk-takers who crave pleasure and individuality. (Ironically, Freud saw religion calming the individual instincts and siding with civilization.[194])

Samuel Huntington, reacting to Fukuyama's *End of History*, predicted a "clash of civilizations": "[I]ntellectuals have not hesitated to proliferate visions of ... the end of history, the return of traditional rivalries between nation states, and the decline of the nation state from the conflicting pulls of tribalism and globalism ... It is my hypothesis that the fundamental source of conflict in this new world will not be primarily ideological or primarily economic. The great divisions among humankind and the dominating source of conflict will be cultural."[195]

Evolution certainly has given humans (and a few other animals) the ability to think rationally, but we all see moral and practical limits in hyper-rationality and hyper-civilization. Most humans understand that life requires a mixture of thought and sensation. Reasonable naturalists make no excuse for using science and spirit in comprehending the universe, and recognize the human specter's interaction with the mysteries of natural order.

As positivists seek out technological substitutes for the rhythms of life and death, naturalists may become increasingly angry and eschew any sort of super-elderly life dominated by electrodes and test tubes. George Bernard Shaw wrote in *The Doctor's Dilemma*: "Do not try to live forever, you will not succeed. Use your health even to the point of wearing it out. That is what it is for. Spend all you have before you die, and do not outlive yourself."[196]

If naturalists do rebel from too much science in determining the fate of man and his environment, some actively may embrace "random mortality"—a reverse of planned life and death. They may become extreme and advocate a return to the Hobbesian brute. Strict theology may join in a milder rebellion, refusing to let science usurp its own holy authority over death. The world may divide with positivists on one side, religionists and naturalists on the other.

Positivists won't necessarily become mad professors who scoff at environmental dangers, promote rampant self-indulgence as part of capitalism, advocate naturalist approaches only when it comes to birth control, or cherry-pick religious tenets when it suits their purpose. Indeed, many likely will remain self-doubters who recognize that nature or God evolved man's mind to conquer problems as they arise.

Those of us forced to choose sides will face a serious dilemma. Few of us remain in perfect health and few of us will refuse the drugs that ease our pains. It's one thing to admire the mountains; it's another to live in them. Few would live in a cave simply to protect nature, or live under the laws of religious fanatics who oppose creeping technology. But even as technology has freed us, it has enslaved us. Whether this slavery can corrupt the breadth and length of our lives is unclear. Nevertheless the extremes may feed the inescapable conflicts of science and nature and religion.

Second Challenge:
Super-Aging May Force Radically New Moral Dilemmas

From every point of view—biological, physical, economic, social, political, moral, naturalist and religious—the elongated lives of some humans can occur only with an offsetting cost to others. If only X number of life slots exist, someone must lose out. Immortality itself never can become fair, with humans sharing equally in the benefits and burdens. The inequality may force civilization to impress some form of birth or death control to limit population. Unlike the relatively easy moral decisions to save innocent children and kill dangerous criminals, we may have to adjudicate life and death based not on crimes, but on simple existence.

Positivists may demand proof of value for the living and promise of value for the unborn—producing an odd form of currency. The currency may evolve into a balanced budget in which life and death are credited and debited according to the same market forces that control tomatoes. Super-aging may become—and perhaps should be—more expensive as overpopulation continues. If people want to live forever, they may have to plead more than self-indulgent reasons. Again, the potential for corruption is enormous. Someone can die for the crime of resting.

If naturalists promote random death as a throwback antidote to positivist selection, they most likely will evade many moral costs of a long life. They may conserve personal survival skills, improve sciences that don't rely on genetic alteration for health and happiness, and follow some non-reactive faith at the same time. In preserving random death, naturalists may avoid the all-pervasive social support enmeshed in keeping old people alive.

Religion may not be so lucky—because for religion, so much a part of traditional society, death belongs not to chance, but to a higher spiritual power. Life comes with moral consequences that impair a human who missteps.[197] When theology attributes all life and death to gods they remove humans from the hard decisions and guilt connected to life and death.[198] But an eye for an eye may be an irresistible call to action even for a religious pacifist. If a higher power shifts from God to a Dr. Mengele or a despotic government, religionists may have no choice but to confront evil with force.

Naturalists and religionists therefore may find themselves either isolated by the crush of moral duty or forced in some way to participate in a selection process. Perhaps everyone will rebel against overpopulation long before life becomes so intolerable; or perhaps everyone may rise up when the choices become too stark to bear. Either way, people may suffer a morality angst in spades.

Third Challenge:
Man May Disrupt Birth

Good positivists will consider the consequences of too much life long before it occurs. Indeed they already are considering the consequences.[199] Obviously, as positivists can turn on creative technology, they can turn it off, leaving the super-elderly to fend for themselves. Denying humans life-saving dialysis, drugs or surgery certainly will curtail populations overnight.

If history and politics are any guides, social positivists first will consider limitations on the addition of new humans before they consider terminating existing people. These limitations will include birth control, abortion, reduced or licensed sexual contact, sterilization and perhaps some sort of genetic alterations to prevent life. China, possibly the most positivist country in the world, has adopted a one child per couple policy to limit new arrivals. The Chinese view high fertility rates as an obstruction to economic growth because too many children burden healthcare, education, law enforcement, housing and the environment for those already alive.

Nevertheless, even the Chinese recognize that blanket application of birth control doesn't work. Many exemptions to the "one child" policy exist, including some connected to wealth, replacement of defective children, the need for an increased number of females, or children born outside of China. Wang Feng, a demographer at the University of California, explains that the "system of exemptions resembles the American tax code in its complexity."

While the policy has limited children, it also has aged the population, shrunk the workforce and skewed the ratio of males to females.[200] Further, the man-made system has led to corruption, including infanticide, forced sterilization and abortions, trafficking in sex, babies and organs, arbitrary enforcement, human rights violations, bribery, racial and housing discrimination. Recently, however, China has heard the wake-up call as it devotes more of its resources from economic growth to elderly welfare. It has begun to consider policy changes.[201]

Prevention of birth requires a full bureaucracy—which as China demonstrates still may not be enough. China augments population control by killing existing humans. While it has avoided paroxysms of genocide, it applies death to violators of minor infractions: the execution rate hovers at 20 times the rest of the world combined.[202] Deviants, such as those who support *Falon Gong*, or the Dali Lama, face short lives. "Death panels" determine the fates of nearly all individuals. While a short-term rationality reigns, selective communalism (i.e. selective communism) has replaced long-view liberality—or even mercy. The capitalism of life and death thrives—but in a collective form. Life can last a long time for a few but at the cost of a short life (or none) for others.

Perhaps we can foresee that for any overpopulated positivist society, humans not only may evolve into a Chinese system and lose the right to produce as many children as they might desire, but they may lose their own lives as well. Producing and maintaining humans no doubt will require the qualities evolution already has promoted: health, security, intelligence. However, unlike nature, committees may work from a script easily tainted by the politics of self-interest and ideology.

Fourth Challenge:
Fear May Mushroom

If science takes over life, it inevitably will take over death. Positivists no doubt will have to institutionalize death to address the effects of overpopulation. Like seasonal deer hunting, murder and suicide may become more widespread (and tolerated) as the state depends on self-help. Because positivist society can't afford to misuse resources, those who fail to justify their existence may be eliminated. While positivists may recognize the need to conserve some risk-taking to preserve economic growth, pervasive failure may result in the massive elimination of life. Only those unafraid or unaware of consequences (or just plain stupid) will venture very far. Security will preoccupy most people.

This cautiousness may lead to fearful, boring lives—similar to existence in the former Soviet Union. Central planning may become a necessary part of positivist life because non-conformity and experimentation carry the life-threatening risk of waste. People may have everything they want, provided they want no more than the government offers. As in Soviet times, government may attempt to limit the material and spiritual desires of humans by propagandizing the failures and excesses of dreamers. A defective human may become nothing more than a broken cog in a highly precise gear. Death of the non-productive may seem genius-like to those concerned with such accuracy, leading to yet more challenges in balancing the moral costs of life and death. The result may become perpetual fear of loss.

Fifth Challenge:
Expulsion May Become the Final Solution

It's possible that positivists may try to send the "unworthy" away before killing them. Perhaps outliers, with the help of technology, can find living space on mountains, underground, at sea, or in space. We already blithely discuss expelling millions of long-term illegal immigrants, even if it causes severe hardship. The possibilities echo the nineteenth century attempts to cleanse the southern U.S. of Native Americans to free up land for white settlers[203] and the twentieth century "living space" debates of those who attempted to reach a "final solution" for unwanted Jews. Indeed, Thomas Jefferson and Abraham Lincoln themselves proposed colonizing freed slaves outside U.S. territory.[204]

In 1830, the U.S. actually passed and enforced the "Indian Removal Act" to make room for whites, leading to the "Trail of Tears."[205] In this despicable part of American history, expansionist policies found that "inferior" humans so hindered land development and the movement of white settlers the government felt compelled to expel Native Americans from their ancestral homes.[206]

A century later, Nazi war criminal Adolf Eichmann, who designed the expulsion of Jews from Austria and Germany, ironically began resettlement efforts in twisted good faith. "The existence of a Jewish reservation at the furthest extremity of the German empire ... was approved and encouraged. ... Eichmann cynically painted a rosy picture of the Jews creating for themselves a new existence in the territory between the San, Bug, and Vistula, where they would be free of the legal restriction imposed upon them in the Third Reich."[207]

Not surprisingly, expulsion often leads to death and genocides. One needs only to look at the eviction of the Chechans from the Caucasus, the ethnic cleansings in Rwanda, the former Yugoslavia, and Darfur. Perhaps positivists may whitewash forced expulsion (leading to expected death) and invoke a moral justification similar to the Turks in their killing of the Armenians: the suppression of civil strife.[208] Or perhaps zealous positivists may speak as honestly as Hitler when he stated, "I have sent to the East my 'Death's Head Units' with the orders to kill without pity or mercy all men, women, and children of Polish race or language. Only in such a way will we win the vital space that we need. Who still talks now about the Armenians?"[209] Or perhaps they may follow Stalin, who killed by expulsions and outright murder as many as 25 million of his own people, stating that "a single death is a tragedy; a million deaths is a statistic."[210]

The sordid history of expulsion explains the genesis of Article 2 of the *UN Convention on the Prevention and Punishment of the Crime of Genocide:* "[G]enocide means any … acts … to destroy … a national, ethnical, racial or religious group, … such [as]: (a) Killing members of the group; … (d) Imposing measures intended to prevent births …; (e) Forcibly transferring children of the group to another group." [211]

Nevertheless, even humane laws designed to preserve defenseless groups could yield to necessity. Removal "rationally" resolves the issue of overpopulation without intentional death. Colonies could form successfully in Antarctica, in abandoned mines, on or under the sea, on the moon, on planets, or even in satellites orbiting planets. By reducing population through resettlement of unwanted groups, the earth population may never reach the levels requiring extreme control—and hubris may be contained. More likely, however, expulsion will become a fig leaf for genocide.

Without doubt, population equilibrium is necessary to preserve freedom. But freedom for whom? For those facing positivist decisions, selectivity becomes an oppressive tool. Some humans may join equally in life on earth and some may not. Among naturalists and religionists, natural selection may dominate, allowing mutts and mistakes; but if positivists prevail, they may employ eugenics and artificial selection to promote a preferred population, and resort to expulsion as the final solution for those they don't prefer.

Sixth Challenge:
Artificial and Natural Selection May Marry

When Dawkins wrote *The Selfish Gene* in 1976 he probably had no idea that he would make the gene a diva of emergence theory. Genes form clusters that produce humans; humans produce cultures; cultures produce cities and political structures—and so on. Each level may not know what it's producing at a higher level, but at the helm genes influence everything.

Genetic manipulation of immortality therefore will change not only the human level, but cultural levels as well. And vice-versa. Society may favor a spry 160-year-old man more than a wheelchair bound 120-year-old who stares zombie-like at a nubile 90-year-old. Society may even encourage the spry man to procreate.

Human genetic inventiveness may link up with nature. Life-creating mutations occur all the time, surprising scientists and doctors with new and often bizarre growths. Killer bacteria and genes have demonstrated their independent creativity by jumping from species. Mad Cow disease, Bird Flu, West Nile disease and AIDS probably originated in non-humans.

Natural selection of artificial genes may take root more quickly than we might imagine. Old age strength and speed, enhanced by super-genes, may launch super-geezers off the starting blocks. But even these superior traits may not satisfy a super-competitive environment: positivist society may demand not only old age intelligence and aggressiveness, but completely new traits such as cat-like vision or even a screen that registers a malfunction with a genetically activated electronic sensor—like a car.[212] The artificial and natural may merge, but one way or another, genes may outfox human strategies of life and death despite the most egalitarian, moral, or even evil intentions of positivists. If this occurs, we can expect virus-like battles with and between our own genes. Perpetually confounding us, when we choose death, our genes may counter with life. When we choose life, our genes may counter with death.

Seventh Challenge:
Will We Remain We?

Can we stop the most radical human traits from proliferating? Certainly if we, as positivists, permit gene alteration in the first place, we may not hesitate to hybridize artificial selection with natural methods. Genes with electronic switches, or light reactors, or that crank up the senses, or enlarge intelligence and creativity, or increase strength, or endure pain, will appeal to us. Humans will continue to vary in size, speed and ability—but perhaps no longer by accident of birth. Discredited eugenics may reappear in a re-energized form. We may design and license humans for specific niches. We may breed dexterous, repetitive-tolerant humans for manufacturing, big-headed humans for intelligence or small humans for space travel. We may manufacture muscular sociopaths for hand-to-hand fighting. A population assigned to live in the arctic may be designed not only like the Inuit, but with genes that tolerate krill if whales and seals become extinct.

We also may breed some people for precise social or cultural niches. Engineering may mark some humans as superior or inferior, and specifically designate those for control and for service. Picking particular humans for immortality may require something like a college admissions committee.

This sort of selection process introduces one moral challenge after another. Will we redesign the human altogether? Will positivists eliminate the perceived ugliness of certain races or the big noses of others? Will positivists prefer only shapely blonde blue eyed girls until blonde jokes make no sense? Which ones will "we" become?

We can imagine the complexities. Every natural function—from apoptosis to cell replication, from conception to death, from thinking to doing, from leading to following—may become our target. Will we delegate the billions of choices to the technicians or bureaucrats, or leave them to chance? If we leave them to technicians and bureaucrats, will our populations simply follow some expedient and fashionable formula? Will women, perhaps left with some free will, want to produce artists instead of doctors or soldiers? If we leave the decisions to voters, will humans become the product of a fickle electorate or will they reflect the computerized will of a central committee?

If we restrict the gene pool, what sort of humans will emerge? As Darwinists and virtually all others have shown, life needs a broad gene pool and the shuffling of genes to avoid impairing variation and adaptation. Will restricting randomness doom the species if another asteroid hits the planet? Will government require that humans know and control the future?

Long before Darwin, Aristotle observed in *Politics*: "That which is common to the greatest number has the least care bestowed upon it." We humans therefore must limit ourselves in order to bestow the most care on the common good. As humans, rather than just common positivists, we have to find the point at which we let nature be nature and God be God. We can hope for continued balance as we stumble through the life and death process. Imposing some ideological purpose on our existence—other than to survive in harmony with nature, God, and ourselves—may be fruitless. There may be a unified purpose in the entire system, but if so, we don't know it; we therefore may have to attribute it to forces larger than any human and leave it at that. Although we can accept that science may uncover deep secrets with strings to the creators—indeed, there already is evidence that mutations may be non-random and purposeful[213]—life just is.

In any event, the peculiar joining of science and nature (and perhaps spirituality) with common purpose ultimately won't resolve the moral questions surrounding a hyper-extended life. The regulatory functions underlying our Faustian desires, born of an instinct to cheat death, no doubt will promote nearly infinite survival strategies like any plant or animal. Some may be moral and some not. Life and death are such powerful allies that even God can't eliminate one without eliminating the other. After millions of years on earth, regulation and purpose have burrowed beneath the surface, and nature requires us to dig for them with both intellectual and emotional tools. Life has made its peace with death—and so must we. The pale rider of death will survive, and he will seek support and purpose from wherever he can find them.

About the Author

Mark Moorstein is a practicing trial lawyer, and senior partner in a Northern Virginia law firm. A Princeton and Temple Law graduate, and member of the bars of various courts, including the U.S. Supreme Court, he has written many legal and non-legal articles, has argued before the highest courts, lectured and taught. At Princeton he wrote for *Triangle* with Scott Berg, Pulitzer Prize writer of *Lindbergh*. For a few years he was a local newspaper columnist, writing both political commentary and humor. He has written two novels, *Red Reflections* and *The Perfect President*, as well as a study of organizational processes, *Frameworks: Conflict in Balance*. He is an instrument-rated pilot, an avid skier, and an award winning photographer. Known for his wit, he once ran and lost a race for the Virginia House of Delegates, explaining his defeat as a result of "someone switching the levers of the voting machines." Mr. Moorstein is married with two adult children.

Endnotes

1   Jay F. Rosenberg, *Reassessing Immortality: The Makropolus Case Revisited*, in *The Good, the Right, Life and Death*, Richard Feldman et al., 2006.

2   David Brooks, *The Geezer's Crusade*, New York Times, February 2, 2010.

3   Ting Zhang, *Elderly Entrepreneurship in an Aging U.S. Economy*, 2008.

4   Titus Lucretius Carus, *De Rerum Natura*, 50 BCE, from the translation of Cyril Bailey, *Lucretius: On the Nature of Things*, 1910.

5   Daniel Callahan, *Setting Limits*, 1987 and 1995.

6   Gina Maranto, *Deoxyribonucleic Acid Trip*, New York Times, August 25, 2002, a review of Gregory Stock's *Redesigning Humans*, 2002.

7   Francis Fukuyama, *Our Posthuman Future*, 2003

8   Martine Rothblatt, *Moot Court Hearing On The Petition Of A Conscious Computer*, 2006, http://www.kurzweilai.net/meme/frame.html?m=4

9   See David Hart, *Christ and Nothing*, The *Humanitas* Project, 2003. Martin Heidegger, *Being and Time*, 1927.

10 Sam Roberts and Sean D. Hamil, *As Deaths Outpace Births, Cities Adjust*, New York Times, May 18, 2008

11 George E. Vaillant, *Aging Well*, 2003.

12 Sherwin Nuland, *Do You Want to Live Forever? Aubrey de Grey thinks he knows how to defeat aging. He's brilliant, but is he nuts? MIT Technology Review*, February 2005

13 The relativity of the observer is not unlike Einsteinian relativity in that even "objective" observers will report different results depending on their location and perspective.

14 Aubrey de Grey and Michael Rae, *Ending Aging: The Rejuvenation Breakthroughs That Could Reverse Human Aging in Our Lifetime*, 2007.

15 De Grey goes so far as to assert that much of current society is in a "trance." See *Aubrey de Grey: Why we age and how to avoid it, Ted*, July 2005, http://www.ted.com/index.php/talks/view/id/39

16 I found this on Amazon.com in connection with de Grey's book, *Ending Aging*, op cite.

17 Olivia Judson, in *An Evolve-By Date*, New York Times, November 25, 2009, writes, "We humans are busily changing the environment for most of the beings on the

planet, and often, we are doing so very fast. ... [I]f we're not careful, many groups will soon be faced with an evolve-by date: if they don't evolve rapidly enough to survive in this changing world, they will vanish. ... Whether a population can evolve to cope with new circumstances depends on how much underlying genetic variation there is: do any individuals in the population have the genes to cope, even barely, with the new environment, or not? If not, everybody dies, and it's game over. If yes, evolution may come to the rescue, improving, as time goes by, the ability of individuals to cope in the new environment. What determines the extent of the underlying genetic variation? Factors such as how big the population is (bigger populations usually contain more genetic variation) and how often mutations occur. ... [T]he initial change the organisms experience [cannot be] ... so severe that no [reproducer] can cope, [or] the population goes extinct." One curious anomaly in the desire for human immortality, the Voluntary Human Extinction Movement, has adopted the motto, "May we live long and die out." In explaining itself, it writes on its website: "VHEMT (pronounced vehement) is a movement ... advanced by people who care about life on planet Earth. We're not just a bunch of misanthropes and anti-social Malthusian misfits, taking morbid delight whenever disaster strikes humans. ... Voluntary human extinction is the humanitarian alternative to human disasters. We don't carry on about how the human race has shown itself to be a greedy, amoral parasite on the once-healthy face of this planet. ... Rather, ... the hopeful alternative to the extinction of millions of species of plants and animals is the voluntary extinction of one species: Homo sapiens—us. Each time another one of us decides not to add another one of us to the burgeoning billions already squatting on this ravaged planet, another ray of hope shines through the gloom. When every human chooses to stop breeding, Earth's biosphere will be allowed to return to its former glory, and all remaining creatures will be free to live, die, evolve ..., and will perhaps pass away, as so many of Nature's 'experiments' have done throughout the eons. It's going to take all of us going." See The Voluntary Human Extinction Movement website, http://www.vhemt.org.

18 Sherwin Nuland, *Do You Want to Live Forever?* Op cite.

19 Message of Pope John Paul II to the staff and residents of the Rennweg Hospice, Vienna, June 21, 1998.

20 While this is the traditional theory, some have disputed it. See e.g. *Bacteria death reduces human hopes of immortality*, *New Scientist* Print Edition, February 5, 2005.http://www.newscientist.com/channel/health/mg18524855.800-bacteria-death-reduces-human-hopes-of-immortality.html. "Many microbiologists had assumed that bacteria effectively never die ... Researchers followed the fortunes of every descendant in nine generations, each grown from a single *Escherichia coli* in 94 separate cultures (that is over 35,000 cells), and have shown that this is not so. Early descendants become steadily wearier and less sprightly. Each rod-shaped *E. coli* has two ends, or 'poles'. As the cell splits, each descendant inherits one 'old' pole and builds one 'new' one. But as a colony expands, the proportion carrying the original old poles gets smaller as waves of descendants with newly

created poles take over. … [D]irect descendants of old-pole cells grew 2 per cent more slowly, were 3 per cent smaller and were more likely to die (*PLoS Biology*, vol 3, e 45). Nature does not seem to do immortality…"

21 See the interesting connection Steven Johnson draws in *The Invention of Air*, 2008. Johnson explains, "The book is centered on the life of Joseph Priestley, the 18th-century British polymath who most people know as the discoverer of oxygen, though the story of that 'discovery' is a very complicated one. What drew me to Priestley originally is another, less contested (and much less recognized) discovery: he was the first person to realize that plants were creating oxygen, in 1771. So in a way Priestley lies at the very beginning of the ecosystems view of the world: the air we breathe is not some inevitable fact of life on earth, but something manufactured as part of a wider system by other organisms on the planet." http://www.stevenberlinjohnson.com/2008/09/the-invention-o.html.

22 Dietrich Stauffer, *Life, Love and Death: Models of Biological Reproduction and Aging*, Institute for Theoretical Physics, Cologne University, April 14, 1999.

23 Carl Jung, *Modern Man in Search of Soul*, 1933

24 Sarah Hrdy, *Evolutionary Context of Human Development: The Cooperative Breeding Model*, MIT Press, 2005

25 K. Hawkes, J.F. O'Connell, N. G. Glurton Jones, H. Alvarez, and E. L. Charnov, *Grandmothering, menopause, and the evolution of human, life histories*, 1997: "Because the risks of mortality accumulate over time, there are fewer [older] individuals … So the force of selection declines with age. … [S]enescence [occurs] because genes have multiple effects. … Genes that have positive effects at younger ages may be favored even though they have negative effects later in life. Those that have positive effects late in life will be disfavored if they have negative early effects. … Grandmothering … [may] strengthen selection against late-acting deleterious mutations by increasing the contribution to descendant gene pools of longer-lived females through the increased reproductive success of their daughters. It would also change the tradeoffs between opposing effects expressed at different ages. Slower senescence generally comes at the cost of reduced fertility at younger ages."

26 J. F. Fries, *Aging, natural death, and the compression of morbidity. New England Journal of Medicine*, July 17, 1980. "The average length of life has risen from 47 to 73 years in this century, but the maximum life span has not increased. Therefore, survival curves have assumed an ever more rectangular form. Eighty per cent of the years of life lost to non-traumatic, premature death have been eliminated, and most premature deaths are now due to the chronic diseases of the later years. Present data allow calculation of the ideal average life span, approximately 85 years. Chronic illness may presumably be postponed by changes in life style, and it has been shown that the physiologic[al] and psychologic[al] markers of aging may be modified. Thus, the average age at first infirmity can be raised, thereby making the morbidity curve more rectangular. Extension of adult vigor far into a fixed life span compresses the period of senescence near the end of life."

27 Steven A. Frank, *Dynamics of Cancer: Incidence, Inheritance, and Evolution*, 2007

28 Ibid. The graph shows age-specific acceleration of mortality by cause of death. Data averaged for the years 1999 and 2000 for non-Hispanic white males in the United States from statistics distributed by the National Center for Health Statistics http://www.cdc.gov/nchs/, Worktable Orig291. The causes of mortality are based on the International Classification of Diseases, Tenth Revision http: // www.cdc.gov/nchs/about/major/dvs/icd10des.htm.

29 Ibid

30 Leonard Hayflick described this limitation in 1965, showing that most cells divide 52 times before they reach their senescent state. See Caleb Ellicott Finch and Leonard Hayflick, *Handbook of the Biology of Aging*, 1977. Also see www. telemere.net, which provides the authority for much of this material.

31 See e.g. Daniel Servan-Schreiber, *Anti-Cancer*, 2007.

32 (1) The loss or degeneration of cells. De Grey suggests the injection of growth factors to stimulate cell division or by periodic transfusion of stem cells. (2) The accumulation of unwanted (a) fat cells, which not only replace muscle but also lead to diabetes, and (b) senescent cells, which accumulate in the cartilage of our joints. De Grey believes scientists will generate or find compounds that will make the cells destroy themselves without affecting others. (3) Mutations in chromosomes: cancer. De Grey proposes to replace stem cells every 10 years with ones engineered not to carry the telomerase gene. (4) Mutations in mitochondria. According to de Grey, mitochondria, the energy producing parts of the cell, contain small amounts of DNA, which are particularly prone to mutations. De Grey proposes putting copies of the mitochondrial genes into the DNA of the nucleus, where they will be safer from mutation-causing influences. The structure of mitochondrial DNA is circular and not linear, and from an evolutionary perspective, mitochondria functions more like original immortal *Monera* cells than advanced mortal human cells (although mitochondria has become a part of human cells). Like any circle, mitochondrial DNA has no beginning or end, which means it has no telomeres. It therefore requires no telomerase to extend its existence. However, research has examined the evolution of mitochondrial DNA (mtDNA) from circular to linear. See e.g. Kovac Lab, http://oldwww.fns.uniba. sk/~kbi/kovlab/telproj.htm "[E]volutionary emergence of linear mtDNA has been accompanied by the adaptation of component(s) of replication machinery to fulfill the needs for complete replication and stabilization of linear genophore. Since the mitochondria of *C.parapsilosis* apparently lack another SSB protein it is possible that mtTBP plays a dual role of mitochondrial SSB and telomere-binding factor." (5) The accumulation of "junk" within the cell. "Junk" results from the cell's breakdown of large molecules. Atherosclerosis reflects one large complication of junk. De Grey proposes to inject into the cells junk eating genes from cell bacteria. (6) The accumulation of "junk" outside the cell. Extracellular fluid, which bathes the cells, may aggregate amyloid, the protein found in Alzheimer's patients. De Grey proposes vaccination with a substance, not yet

developed, that will stimulate the immune system to consume the junk. (7) Cross-links in proteins outside the cell. Chemical bonds called "cross-links" form between independent molecules in the exracellular fluid, causing a loss of elasticity or a thickening of tissue, which, for example, may lead to high blood pressure. De Grey again hopes to identify chemicals or enzymes capable of breaking the cross-links without damaging anything else.

33 Predators, however, seem to curtail the population of lemmings even more than the hazards of migration. One study explains that "[t]hough the impact of the fox, the owl and the skua [similar to seagulls] is spectacular in summer, it is the fourth predator, the stoat [a short-tailed weasel], that really sets the pace of lemming dynamics. The stoat is a resident predator, hunting lemmings ... under [the] snow in winter. The rate of reproduction of the stoat is, however, much lower than ... the lemming, and hence the numbers of the stoat lag behind the ... prey. But when the other three predators have stopped, the lemming population increases, the stoat ... catch[es] up and ... [becomes] the main culprit [behind] the crash of the lemming population ... Then follows the collapse of the stoat population itself, and a new cycle is started." Ilkka Hanski, *Predators drive the lemming cycle in Greenland*, University of Helsinki, October 31, 2003, http://www.innovations-report.com/html/reports/environment_ sciences/report-22885.html

34 While the loss of lemmings might seem insignificant (except as a loss of a useful metaphor), bees already have begun to disappear in many industrialized nations, leaving fruit and flower production in tatters. See e.g. *Nation Honey Board Funds Research for 'Colony Collapse Disorder,'* http://www.beedisorder.com/

35 Had the earth avoided an asteroid hit, or somehow remained more stable during natural calamities, perhaps intelligent life would have descended from dinosaurs. For a humorous romp in this fantasy, see Eric Garcia's novel, *Anonymous Rex*, 1999.

36 Freud's major breakthrough came in *Beyond the Pleasure Principle*, published in 1920, in which, based on his observations, he concluded that a death force, as a "repetition compulsion," counteracted the desire for pleasure. As we will note later, the life and death forces may be measured by heat at a cellular level and dollars at a social level. If so, there may exist discrete ratios of 2:1, suggesting that life requires equal force to stop death and another dose to rise above it.

37 See Stephen Hawking, *A Brief History of Time*, 1988.

38 Message at Rennweg Hospice, op cite.

39 See Beverly Peterson and Stephen C. Stearns, *Watching, from the Edge of Extinction*, 2000.

40 Darwin and others (e.g. S.M. Stanley) have drawn the relationship between speciation and population size. Generally, the greater the rates of speciation, the greater the chance of extinction. See Stephen Jay Gould, *The Structure of Evolutionary Theory*, 2002.

41 The literature of science and politics already evidences the controversy. Sarah Palin's 2009 comments about national healthcare imposing "death panels" shows

that some already are concerned with unnatural selection. Scientists themselves routinely debate the ethical limits of social control.

42 Steven Johnson, *Emergence: The Connected Lives of Ants, Brains, Cities and Software,* 2001

43 John Markoff, *The Coming Superbrain, New York Times,* May 23, 2009.

44 See e.g. John F. Haught, Francisco José Ayala, *Science and Religion in Search of Cosmic Purpose,* 2001, especially the chapter by Francisco Ayala, *Darwin and the Teleology of Nature.*

45 This form of the theory has been derived by countless writers. However, according to Enrico Fermi in *Thermodyanmics,*1956, the second law has two pure forms: "A transformation whose only final result is to transform into work heat extracted from a source which is at the same temperature throughout is impossible. (Postulate of Lord Kelvin)" and "A transformation whose only final result is to transfer heat from a body at a given temperature to a body at a higher temperature is impossible. (Postulate of [Rudolf] Clausius.)"

46 Einstein believed that entropy probably explained all organization. Einstein stated "[A law] is more impressive the greater the simplicity of its premises, the more different are the kinds of things it relates, and the more extended its range of applicability. Therefore, the deep impression which classical thermodynamics made on me. It is the only physical theory of universal content, which I am convinced, that within the framework of applicability of its basic concepts will never be overthrown." M. J. Klein, *Thermodynamics in Einstein's Universe, Science,* 157, 1967.

47 Sarah Hrdy suggests that "cooperative breeding" explains a longer life past the reproductive period: grandmothers and others (she calls "allomothers") who protect children also protect their own genes, allowing for slower maturation, quality over quantity, and the development of social complexity. See e.g. S.B. Hrdy, *Mother Nature: Maternal Instincts and How They Shape the Human Species,* 1999.

48 Sabrina Büttner, Tobias Eisenberg, Eva Herker, Didac Carmona-Gutierrez, Guido Kroemer, and Frank Madeo, *Why yeast cells can undergo apoptosis: death in times of peace, love, and war,* 2006.

49 Ibid.

50 Thomas Hobbes, *Leviathan,* 1660.

51 See http://en.wikiquote.org/wiki/Will_Rogers

52 Curiously, though, the *New York Times* on July 18, 2008 printed a front page article *Rise Seen in Medical Efforts to Treat the Very Old.* One notable part states, "Dr. Friedman said Mrs. Homer's [104-year-old] heart is much stronger since the operation, and that her health is generally good—akin to that of, perhaps, a 94-year-old. Her only hospitalization since the procedure has been a brief stay for pneumonia, he said. 'She might have passed away in 2004, so theoretically Medicare wouldn't have been putting a lot of money out,' he noted. 'But our

goal, as a society, hopefully, is quality of life with some kind of cost we can afford.'"

53 See *A World of Methuselahs* in the *Economist* monograph *The Slow Burning Fuse*, June 2009,

54 In January, 2009 an unemployed American woman, who already had six in-vitro children, gave birth to eight more in-vitro babies. "The Southern California woman who gave birth to octuplets last week told *Today's* Ann Curry in an exclusive interview that growing up as an only child, she had always dreamed of having 'a huge family.' She also denied charges that she was irresponsible to have so many babies—especially with six other children already at home." See Mike Celizic, *Octuplet mom defends her 'unconventional' choices*, Feb. 6, 2009. http://www.msnbc.msn.com/id/29038814/

55 Sometimes in order to conserve workers and reproduction. For example, Germany provides cradle-to-grave health benefits, but avoids military risks to the point of endangering itself. Also see John Pomfret, *A Long Wait at the Gate to Greatness*, *Washington Post*, July 27, 2008: "China's demographics stink. No country is aging faster than the People's Republic, which is on track to become the first nation in the world to get old before it gets rich. Because of the Communist Party's notorious one-child-per-family policy, the average number of children born to a Chinese woman has dropped from 5.8 in the 1970s to 1.8 today—below the rate of 2.1 that would keep the population stable. Meanwhile, life expectancy has shot up, from just 35 in 1949 to more than 73 today. Economists worry that as the working-age population shrinks, labor costs will rise, significantly eroding one of China's key competitive advantages. Worse, Chinese demographers such as Li Jianmin of Nankai University now predict a crisis in dealing with China's elderly, a group that will balloon from 100 million people older than 60 today to 334 million by 2050, including a staggering 100 million age 80 or older. How will China care for them? With pensions? Fewer than 30 percent of China's urban dwellers have them, and none of the country's 700 million farmers do. And China's state-funded pension system makes Social Security look like Fort Knox."

56 See, e.g. George H. Taylor and Chad Southards, *Long-term Climate Trends and Salmon Population*, April, 1997, http://www.ocs.orst.edu/reports/climate_fish.html

57 JR Speakman, *Body size, energy metabolism and lifespan, Journal of Experimental Biology*, 208, 2005. "Bigger animals live longer. ... [A]cross species a gram of tissue on average expends about the same amount of energy before it dies regardless of whether that tissue is located in a shrew, a cow, an elephant or a whale. This fact led to the notion that aging and lifespan are processes regulated by energy metabolism rates and that elevating metabolism will be associated with premature mortality—the rate of living theory. The free-radical theory of aging provides a potential mechanism that links metabolism to aging phenomena, since oxygen free radicals are formed as a by-product of oxidative phosphorylation. Despite this potential synergy in these theoretical approaches,

the free-radical theory has grown in stature while the rate of living theory has fallen into disrepute. This is primarily because comparisons made across classes (for example, between birds and mammals) do not conform to the expectations, and even within classes there is substantial interspecific variability in the mass-specific expenditure of energy per lifespan."

58 Thomas Malthus, *An Essay on the Principle of Population*, 1798. The "moral restraint" Malthus refers to is somewhat oblique, but it seems to mean old fashioned sex, not public policy: "[M]oral restraint [which the reader will recollect the confined sense in which I use the term] does not at present prevail much among the male part of society ... [A] much larger proportion of women pass a considerable part of their lives in the exercise of this virtue than in past times and among uncivilized nations ... But however this may be ... it may be considered ... as the most powerful of the check, which in modern Europe keeps down the population to the level of the means of subsistence."

59 Jared Diamond, *Collapse: How Societies Choose to Fail or Succeed*, 2005.

60 See e.g. Natalie Jackson, *Population ageing in a nutshell: a phenomenon in four dimensions,* Monash University, Centre for Population and Urban Research, 2007

61 Introduction, Paragraph 2, *United Nations Report of the Second World Assembly on Aging*, Madrid, April 8-12, 2002. The same paragraph ends with this understated warning: "Such a global demographic transformation has profound consequences for every aspect of individual, community, national and international life. Every facet of humanity will evolve: social, economic, political, cultural, psychological and spiritual."

62 *Suffer the Little Children*, subpart of *A Slow Burning Fuse*, the *Economist* monograph, June 2009.

63 One scenario suggests that older populations with highly developed intellectual skills will out-perform populations equipped only with basic physical strength—both in production and war. As societies age, they will have to rely on technology, robots and wisdom to overcome societies filled only with young workers and fighters. Rather than sacrifice their scarce youth for back-breaking labor or military service, older societies will safeguard their young for limited reproduction, for mastering the sophisticated mental skills necessary to apply technology, and for outfoxing less sophisticated societies. Of course, the fittest societies will combine both physical and mental strength: the young and intelligent.

64 In Paragraph 77, Objective 4, Action (c), the UN Report, op cite, encourages countries to "[p]romote self-care in older persons and maximize their strengths and abilities within health and social services." However, a far more comprehensive analysis in the *Economist, A Slow Burning Fuse*, op cite, recognizes the problems of an accumulating elderly population: "As more people retire, and fewer younger ones take their place, the labor force will shrink, so output growth will drop unless productivity increases faster. Since the remaining workers will be older, they may actually be less productive."

65 In an email to me dated June 5, 2009, Marian Starkey, the communications manager of Population Connection, wrote, "Population Connection seeks to improve the quality of life for everyone—including the elderly. We advocate stabilizing population via eliminating unintended pregnancy, not by capping lifespan."

66 Jacqueline Kasun, *The War Against Population: The Economics and Ideology of World Population Control*, 1999

67 The Hutus needed only the slightest spark to launch their genocide. Even otherwise peaceful citizens joined in the killing. See *Rwanda: How the genocide happened*, BBC, December 18, 2008, http://news.bbc.co.uk/1/hi/world/africa/1288230.stm: "Between April and June 1994, an estimated 800,000 Rwandans were killed in the space of 100 days. Most of the dead were Tutsis—and most of those who perpetrated the violence were Hutus. ... Within hours, recruits were dispatched all over the country to carry out a wave of slaughter. ... The early organisers included military officials, politicians and businessmen, but soon many others joined in the mayhem. Encouraged by the presidential guard and radio propaganda, an unofficial militia group called the Interahamwe (meaning those who attack together) was mobilised. At its peak, this group was 30,000-strong. Soldiers and police officers encouraged ordinary citizens to take part. In some cases, Hutu civilians were forced to murder their Tutsi neighbours by military personnel. Participants were often given incentives, such as money or food, and some were even told they could appropriate the land of the Tutsis they killed."

68 See the excellent monograph from the *Economist, A Slow Burning* Fuse, June 27, 2009.

69 According to a number of studies, dichloroacetic acid ("DCA") may be the beginning of cheap anti-cancer compounds. Cancer cells rely on glycolysis rather than oxidation for energy. A study published in January 2007 by researchers at the University of Alberta, testing DCA on *in vitro* cancer cell lines and a rat model, found that DCA restored mitochondrial function, thus restoring apoptosis, killing cancer cells *in vitro*, and shrinking the tumors in the rats. DCA induces apoptosis, decreases proliferation, and inhibits tumor growth, without apparent toxicity. S. Bonnet, SL Archer, J Allalunis-Turner, et al., *A mitochondria-K+ channel axis is suppressed in cancer and its normalization promotes apoptosis and inhibits cancer growth, Cancer Cell*. 2007 Jan;11(1):37-51.

70 Nuland, in his article on de Grey, suggests that the morality of life will shift with the science that overcomes death: man at first will feel pride extending life, but feel guilt for failing to extend all lives. Nuland: "[W]hat would seem the obvious objection that such moral codes assume our current life span and not one lasting thousands of years? [De Grey]: '*It's an incremental thing. It's not a question of how long life should be, but whether the end of life should be hastened by action or inaction.*' And there it is—the ultimate leap of ingenious argumentation that would do a sophist proud: by our inaction in not pursuing the possible

opportunity of extending life for thousands of years, we are hastening death." Sherwin Nuland, *Do You Want to Live Forever?* Op cite.

71 John-Paul Sartre, *Being and Nothingness*, 1956. Sartre asks, "Is Nothingness not in fact simple identity with itself, complete emptiness, absence of determinations and of content?" Who wouldn't be frightened of Nothingness? Sartre spends considerable times and effort establishing the superiority of Being.

72 Mark 8:36.

73 Nicholas Wade, *Stem Cells May Be Key to Cancer*, New York Times, February 21, 2006

74 The 2009 Iranian elections became a text book case of imbalance: a large segment, but not the majority, of the voting public objected to the sitting president. Instead of tolerating dissent, the government killed and prosecuted protestors, leading to the creation of more dissent.

75 See Jared Diamond's description of this process in *Collapse*. In Prince William County, Virginia, where I live, the local politics disfavors illegal immigration because of the cost of healthcare and schooling for immigrant children. The unintended consequences of forcing out immigrants has been a sharp increase in mortgage foreclosures, a decrease in business, and a complete reversal of the growth fueling many of the benefits for the local community.

76 See e.g. a BBC report called *Aging Population Fuels Debate*, 2000, http://news.bbc.co.uk/1/hi/health/background_briefings/euthanasia/331125.stm

77 Carl Jung, *The Archetypes and the Collective Unconscious*, 1954.

78 See the detailed explanation by David Grant Stewart, Sr., *The Ten Commandments Translation*, 2007, http://www.72languages.com/tencommandments.php. "חצרתתאל Thou shalt not commit murder: אל Not; ת Imperative prefix; חצר Murder, shatter, slay. This word does not connote the acts of a soldier in wartime, nor of a butcher in a butcher shop. It means specifically the deliberate, premeditated murder of an innocent person without legal or moral justification"

79 Deuteronomy 30:19. Buddhists also make clear that life is better than death—provided that the living don't act like vegetables. In his discourses in *Dhammapada*, the Buddha states, "Watchfulness is the path of immortality: unwatchfulness is the path of death. Those who are watchful never die: those who do not watch are already dead."

80 Kant's quote, from *Groundwork of the Metaphysic of Morals*,1785, is "*Handel so, daß du die Menschheit sowohl in deiner Person, als auch in der Person eines jeden anderen jederzeit zugleich als Zweck, niemals bloß als Mittel brauchest.*" The common translation is "Act in such a way that you treat humanity, whether in your own person or in the person of any other, always at the same time as an end and never merely as a means to an end." A less stilted translation might be, "Treat humanity as an end and not merely as a means to an end," i.e. don't use people.

81 Plato, *Apology*, 31.

82 Jame Lovelock, *Gaia: A New Look at Life on Earth,* 1979.

83 See an interesting discussion of Einstein's desire to maintain balance through the "cosmological constant" in *God and the New Cosmology: The Anthropic Design Argument* by Michael Anthony Corey, 1993.

84 See Thomas Kuhn, *The Structure of Scientific Revolutions*, 1962, and my *Frameworks: Conflict in Balance*, 2004.

85 As noted later, Richard Dawkins in his *The Selfish Gene*, 1990, argues that complex life emanates from the control of genes, as if they had purpose and even sentience.

86 Matt Ridley, *Genome*, 2000.

87 A. Dalgleish, *The Relevance of Non-linear Mathematics (Chaos Theory) to the Treatment of Cancer*, QJ Med 92:247-359, 1999.

88 Richard V. Sole, Jordi Bascompte, and Susann C. Manrubia, *Extinction: Bad Genes or Weak Chaos*, Santa Fe Institute, 1996

89 A. Dalgleish, op cite.

90 Adam Lomnicki and Ryszard Korona, *Evolution: Harmonizing Chaos*, Jagiellonian University, Krakow, 2006

91 Michael S. Lewis-Beck, William G. Jacoby, Helmut Norpoth, and Herbert F. Weisberg, *The American Voter Revisited*, 2008. Libby Copeland, a writer for the *Washington Post*, on July 24, 2008, wrote, "Their conclusion—that the voter is pretty much the same dismally ill-informed creature he was back then—continues a decades-long debate about whether Americans are as clueless as they sound."

92 Auguste Comte, *The Positive Philosophy of Auguste Comte, Freely Translated and Condensed by Harriet Martineau*. AMS Press. (1974 reprint; original work published in 1855, New York, NY, Calvin Blanchard)

93 Ibid.

94 See, e.g. *Encarta Dictionary*

95 Genesis 1:1 and 1:2. Buddhists also define the universe both materially and spiritually, but through the eyes of the Buddha: "[The shape of the universe] is not intended to be a description of how ordinary humans perceive their world; rather, it is the universe as seen through the *divyacak us (Pāli: dibbacakkhu)*, the 'divine eye' by which a Buddha or an *arhat* who has cultivated this faculty can perceive all of the other worlds and the beings arising (being born) and passing away (dying) within them, and can tell from what state they have been reborn and into what state they will be reborn. The cosmology has also been interpreted in a symbolical or allegorical sense ... Buddhist cosmology can be divided into two related kinds: spatial cosmology, which describes the arrangement of the various worlds within the universe, and temporal cosmology, which describes how those worlds come into existence, and how they pass away." http://en.wikipedia.org/wiki/Buddhist_cosmology

96 Modern naturalist philosophy has a branch that explores spiritualism (known as "metaphysical naturalism," sometimes called "philosophical naturalism" or "ontological naturalism"). Comte used the term "metaphysics" to include all

naturalism. With recent theories of physics addressing multiple dimensions, strings, and alternate universes, physics and metaphysics do seem to overlap. The modern metaphysical naturalist has few qualms about venturing into spiritualism. Without going into the extensive history of the separation of "methodological naturalism" from "metaphysical naturalism," the point can be summed up by Francis Bacon's reliance on investigation and logic rather than supernatural forces to explain the workings of the material world. See, e.g. Thomas Kuhn's *The History of Scientific Revolutions*.

97 C.S. Lewis, in *Miracles*, 1946, asserts that nature doesn't fill reality. Nature is a "partial system within reality." Reality includes items that exist, but are "supernatural" and permit unexplained miracles.

98 See e.g. F. M. Cornford, *Plato's Theory of Knowledge: The Theaetetus and The Sophist*, 1935.

99 For an interesting discussion of this point, see *Where is Christ's Body? Notes from Off-Center*, November 8, 2008, http://notes-from-offcenter.com/2008/11/08/where-is-christs-body: "What is a fully human resurrection? Two views persist that have equal scriptural premise. 1. When human beings die, the immortal soul departs straight for heaven. If heaven is some place within the structure of space-time, then we could conceivably visit it in our super fast spaceship (even Star Trek V played with this idea only to find that "God" and "Eden" was just a planet with a really selfish life form who wanted a ship). The more traditional view would understand heaven as some place outside of space-time akin to the *Cloud of Unknowing*—it is a "place" that has only analogy *via negativa* to anything we experience within the structure of space-time. 2. When humans die the soul rests until the general resurrection of the dead for all at which point the last judgment will occur which is widely attested in numerous source of Scripture. Certainly for the Greek sensibility towards matter, the resurrection of the body would not be part of this general resurrection. This would be a resurrection of the immaterial part of the human being, namely the soul. The same issues apply as above with heaven - the location of the final resting place of the human being. The question here is if this is a fully human resurrection."

100 See e.g. Daniel Pals, *Eight Theories of Religion*, 2008.

101 The rewards and punishments of the Bible aren't subtle. Romans 6:23 provides: "The wages of sin is death; but the gift of God is eternal life through Jesus Christ our Lord." Also see e.g. the *Psychology of Religion and Death*, http://everything2.com/e2node/Psychology%2520of%2520Religion%2520and%2520Death.

102 Francis Fukuyama, *The End of History and the Last Man*, 1992. Fukuyama writes that "The unfolding of modern natural science has had a uniform effect on all societies that have experienced it, for two reasons. In the first place, technology confers decisive military advantages ... Second [it] establishes a uniform horizon of economic production possibilities. Technology makes possible limitless accumulation of wealth, and thus the satisfaction of an ever-expanding set of human desires."

103 *Saudi Publications on Hate Ideology Invade American Mosques*, Center for

Religious Freedom, Freedom House, 1319 18th Street, NW, Washington, DC 20036, 2005, citing Al-Aql, Dr. Nasir. *Whoever Imitates a People, He is from Them*. Riyadh: Institute of Islamic and Arabic Sciences in America, 1991. Collected from Masjid Al-Islam.

104 Barack Obama, *Speech at Cairo University*, June 4, 2009

105 From *Planet About To Be Recycled - Your Only Chance To Survive - Leave With Us*, Edited Transcript of Videotape, October 5, 1996, http://www.heavensgate.com/mis/vt100596.htm

106 http://www.islamonline.net/servlet/Satellite?pagename=IslamOnline-English-Ask_Scholar/FatwaE/FatwaE&cid=1119503544298

107 See, e.g. *What is Hare Krishna?* "Having lost touch with our original, pure consciousness we are trying to achieve permanent happiness within a temporary world. Our attempts produce karmic reactions which cause us to remain within this world for repeated lifetimes *(samsara)*. http://www.iskcon.org.uk/faqs/source.html

108 *The Ch'ing Ching Ching, The Words of Lao Chün. Sacred Texts of Tao*. http://www.sacred-texts.com/tao/ttx/ttx08.htm

109 Christ in John 14:13 refers to the "Spirit of Truth." Pope John Paul II writes in *How Much More Will the Father in Heaven Give the Holy Spirit to Those Who Ask Him?* 2004, "Jesus adds: 'But the Counselor, the Holy Spirit, whom the Father will send in my name, he will teach you all things, and bring to your remembrance all that I have said to you' (John 14:26). The Holy Spirit will be … always present in their midst—even though invisible—as the teacher of the same Good News that Christ proclaimed. The words 'he will teach' and 'bring to remembrance' mean not only that he, in his own particular way, will continue to inspire the spreading of the Gospel of salvation but also that he will help people to understand the correct meaning of the content of Christ's message; they mean that he will ensure continuity and identity of understanding in the midst of changing conditions and circumstances. The Holy Spirit, then, will ensure that in the Church there will always continue the same truth which the Apostles heard from their Master."

110 Richard Dawkins, *Is Science a Religion?* American Humanist Association, January/February 1997.

111 Science, according to Thomas Kuhn in *The Structure of Scientific Revolutions*, also may be less a matter of "truth" than probability. It also may be analogous to a mathematical limit in which "reality" approaches the limits of nature.

112 See Walter Isaacson, *Einstein: His Life and Universe*, 2007.

113 See e.g. Elias Kiritsis, *String Theory in a Nutshell*, 2007

114 http://thinkexist.com/quotation/imagination_is_more_important_than_knowledge-for/260230.html

115 Although Sartre's *Being and Nothingness*, op cite, explains the Hegelian aspects of "negative" of existence, I am simply referring to the basic tendency of any

human to wonder about the purpose of an object: "Why is that tree standing there? Why does the sun shine?"

116 Vivianne Crowley, *Jung: A Journey of Transformation: Exploring His Life and Experiencing His Ideas,* 2000.

117 From the poem *High Flight*, John Gillespie Magee, Jr., 1941. Magee was 19 years old when he wrote the poem.

118 "[Darwin, in *The Descent of Man*] first sets the context by reminding the reader that sounds generally evolve for reproductive functions: 'Although the sounds emitted by animals of all kinds serve many purposes, a strong case can be made out, that the vocal organs were primarily used and perfected in relation to the propagation of the species' (Darwin, 1871, p. 875). He reviews as examples the sounds of frogs, toads, tortoises, alligators, birds, mice, and gibbons, which are produced only in the breeding season, usually only by males, but sometimes by both sexes. He then reviews the anatomy of sound perception to argue that the capacity to perceive musical notes could easily have begun as a side-effect of the capacity to distinguish noises in general: 'an ear capable of discriminating noises—and the high importance of this power to all animals is admitted by every one—must be sensitive to musical notes.' (Darwin, 1871, p. 877)" Wallin, B. Merker, & S. Brown (Eds.), *The Origins of Music*, MIT Press.

119 Op cite

120 There is no doubt that many animals can imagine and anticipate events. See e.g. Robert W. Mitchell, *Pretending and Imagination in Animals and Children*, 2002

121 Aristotle, *Nichomachean Ethics*, 1170a25 ff (Book 9, Section 9), 350 BC

122 This quote has also been attributed to Einstein.

123 Jean-Dominique Bauby, *The Diving Bell and the Butterfly*, 1997.

124 Soren Kierkegaard, *The Concept of Dread*, 1844

125 Jonathan Swift, *Gulliver's Travels*, 1727

126 Reading the German idealists is sometimes like deciphering an electrical diagram. The basic idea is that things "are" and things "should be" ("sollen" in German). The subjunctive gives rise to any number of philosophical concepts—including being, freedom, morality, absolutism, idealism, utopianism, and, of course, their opposites.

127 The French seem to own the existentialism that ponders the mismatch of physical and intellectual freedom. Voltaire said that if God didn't exist, someone would have to invent him to explain the creativity in the universe. Writers, soldiers and thinkers like Voltaire, Napoleon General Edouard-Jean-Baptiste Milhaud (who quipped that if death didn't exist someone would have to invent it), Sartre, Camus, and Simone de Beauvoir collectively question whether freedom of thought is enough to sustain life.

128 Homer, *Odyssey*, ca. 800 BC, Book 18, translation by Robert Fitzgerald, 1961.

129 http://nigelwarburton.typepad.com/virtualphilosopher/2007/11/podcast-intervi.html

130 Jean Paul Sartre, *Being and Nothingness,* op cite.

131 Albert Camus, *Death of Sisyphus*, 1942.

132 Ayn Rand, *Capitalism: The Unknown Ideal*, 1946.

133 Ayn Rand, *Conservatism: An Obituary*, 1960, from a lecture given at Princeton.

134 Moral restraint, especially, imposes a collective conscience on society without governmental intervention. See Kristina Arp's discussion in *The Bonds of Freedom*, 2001. Simone de Beauvoir distinguishes "ontological freedom," which relates to "the complete freedom of thought," from "moral freedom," which paradoxically may be a *self-restraint* that converts thought into action. (Many vehemently dispute that moral freedom even exists or puts the brakes on anything. Michael Gross, for example, writes that "[t]he most politically competent individuals are, most often, the least morally competent." Michael L. Gross, *Ethics and Activism*, 1997.)

135 See *Girl, 13, put into care for wanting to sail solo around the world*, guardian. co.uk, August 28, 2009, http://www.guardian.co.uk/world/2009/aug/28/laura-dekker-solo-sail-court

136 Ayn Rand, *Capitalism: The Unknown Ideal*, op cite.

137 Friedrich von Hayek, *The Road to Serfdom*, 1944.

138 Even if we legislated the right to go back in time, for example, we still would find ourselves blocked by forces we are powerless to overcome. John A. Gowan writes in *Feynman Diagrams and "Time's Arrow,"* http://www.people.cornell. edu/pages/jag8/index.html, revised March 2006, that "On page 118-119 of his biography of Richard Feynman *'Genius'* ... James Gleick recounts a meeting between [Richard] Feynman, J. A. Wheeler, and Albert Einstein in which the three of them agree that the fundamental equations describing the absorption and emission of light waves by atoms are symmetric with respect to the sign of the time parameter—that is, there is no directionality of 'time's arrow' at the microscopic level of phenomena; it is only at the macroscopic level that the irreversible character of time begins to assert itself, and then for no other reason than probability."

139 Plato, *Apology*, 21

140 See Plato's *Theaetetus*, section 152a. *Sextus Empiricus* (*Adv. math.* 7.60) .

141 Rene Descartes, *Meditations on First Philosophy*, in *The Philosophical Writings of René Descartes*, 1641, translated by J. Cottingham, R. Stoothoff and D. Murdoch, Cambridge: Cambridge University Press, 1984.

142 "*Cogito ergo sum*," or in Descartes' French, "*Je pense donc je suis*." Rene Descartes, *Discourse on Method*, 1637.

143 Aristotle, *Nichomachean Ethics*, 1170a25 ff (Book 9, Section 9), 350 BC

144 Plato, *Theaetetus*, 151d7-e3, 369 BC

145 Sigmund Freud, *The Uncanny*, 1919. Freud refers extensively to the work of Otto Rank.

146 Lucretius, *De Rerum Natura*, op cite.

147 Science met spirituality when Duncan MacDougall, M.D. calculated in 1907

(about the time Einstein was contemplating the special theory of relativity) that by weighing patients just before and after death, the soul has a mass of about 21 grams. In an article in *American Medicine*, April, 1907, with the title, *Hypothesis Concerning Soul Substance Together with Experimental Evidence of The Existence of Such Substance*, he wrote: "If personal continuity after ... bodily death is a fact, if the psychic functions continue to exist as a separate individually or personality after the death of brain and body, then such personality can only exit as a space occupying body, unless the relations between space objective and space notions in our consciousness, established in our consciousness by heredity and experience, are entirely wiped out at death and a new set of relations between space and consciousness suddenly established in the continuing personality. This would be an unimaginable breach in the continuity of nature. It is unthinkable that personality and consciousness continuing personal identity should exist ... and yet not occupy space. It is impossible to represent in thought that which is not space-occupying, as having personality; for that would be equivalent to thinking that nothing had become ... something, that emptiness had personality, that space itself was more than space, all of which are contradictions and absurd. Since therefore it is necessary to the continuance of conscious life and personal identity after death, that they must have for a basis that which is space-occupying, or substance, the question arises has this substance weight, is it ponderable? The essential thing is that there must be a substance as the basis of continuing personal identity and consciousness, for without space-occupying substance, personality or a continuing conscious ego after bodily death is unthinkable."

148 E.g. Gregg Braden, *The God Code*, 2004. According to a summary by Linda Brown, "The book is based on the fact that the basic elements of DNA—hydrogen, nitrogen, oxygen and carbon translate directly to key letters of both the Hebrew and Arabic alphabets and that in both alphabets they spell the name of God. According to Bragg, what this means is that the letters of God's ancient name 'are encoded as the genetic formation in every cell, of every life.' The message that is revealed when the chemistry of our cells is translated into the letters of ancient Hebrew is 'God/Eternal within the body.' This message is the same regardless of our race, color, religion or anything else. The author states, 'The odds that this relationship has occurred by chance are approximately 1 in 200,000.'"

149 Carl Jung, *Modern Man in Search of Soul*, 1933

150 Knowledge is the mainstay of Gnosticism. See *Catholic Encyclopedia*: "[Gnosticism is t]he doctrine of salvation by knowledge. This definition, based on the etymology of the word (*gnosis* "knowledge", *gnostikos*, "good at knowing"), is correct as far as it goes, but it gives only one, though perhaps the predominant, characteristic of Gnostic systems of thought. Whereas Judaism and Christianity, and almost all pagan systems, hold that the soul attains its proper end by obedience of mind and will to the Supreme Power, i.e. by faith and works, it is markedly peculiar to Gnosticism that it places the salvation of the soul merely in the possession of a quasi-intuitive knowledge of the mysteries of

the universe and of magic formulae indicative of that knowledge. Gnostics were 'people who knew', and their knowledge at once constituted them a superior class of beings, whose present and future status was essentially different from that of those who, for whatever reason, did not know."

151 Corinthians 6:2

152 Bernard Spinoza, *Ethics*,1677

153 Aristotle, *Metaphysics* 1011b25. Also see *The Correspondence Theory of Truth*, Stanford Dictionary of Philosophy, http://plato.stanford.edu/entries/truth-correspondence.

154 Plato, *Apology*, 21

155 Carl Jung, *Modern Man in Search of Soul*, 1933

156 Jean Paul Sartre, *Being and Nothingness,* op cite.

157 Anna Quindlen, *How Reading Changed My Life*, 1998. The entire quote is "Ignorance is death. A closed mind is a catafalque."

158 Johnny Welch, *The Puppet* (in Spanish), 1999. "The poem turned out to be the work of an obscure Mexican ventriloquist named Johnny Welch. Welch had written the poem for his puppet sidekick 'Mofles,' but somehow his name had been replaced by the name of the Nobel Prize winning author." See http://www.museumofhoaxes.com/marquez.html.

159 A quote floating through the Department of Defense in 2005 went something like this: "We know what we know. We know that we don't know some things. We don't know, however, what we don't know." Donald Rumsfeld, the infamous Secretary of Defense under George W. Bush, mangled it this way: "There are known knowns, there are things that we know. There are known unknowns, that is to say that there are things that we now know we don't know. But there are unknown unknowns, there are things we do not know we don't know, and each year we discover a few more of those unknown unknowns." From the *Washington Post*, November 23, 2007.

160 See, e.g. Robert Belshaw, V. Pereira, A. Katzourakis, G. Talbot, J. Paces, A. Burt, M. Tristem, *Long-term reinfection of the human genome by endogenous retroviruses*, National Academy of Sciences, USA 101 (14), April 2004

161 I recall a radio talk show in 2008 in which a Generation X member railed against supporting elderly baby boomers because they "experimented with drugs," were self-absorbed, demanded too much, and deserved all the misery of old age.

162 See Brainy Quote, http://www.brainyquote.com/quotes/authors/g/george_s_patton.html

163 Matthew 5:43-44

164 John Stuart Mill, *Utilitarianism*, 1863

165 Frederick H. Russell, *Just War in the Middle Ages,*1975.

166 This estimate is based on the Historical Tables cited above and information from the World Health Organization (http://www.who.int/whosis/whostat2007_6healthsystems_nha.pdf). The figures are not intended to be exact,

but only to demonstrate a relationship. Also see UC Atlas on Inequality, http://ucatlas.ucsc.edu/health/expenditure.html, which notes: "Global inequality in health care spending is large. … [T]he countries in the highest quintile (20%) spend more than 16 times the amount spent by the lowest quintile. The highest 5% of the countries spend 4492% of the lowest quintile. This … includes both government and personal expenditures. Despite the wide gaps, higher spending on health care does not necessarily prolong lives. In 2000, the United States spent more on health care than any other country in the world: an average of $4,500 per person. … Nevertheless, average U.S. life expectancy ranks 27th in the world, at 77 years. … Countries with higher spending generally have longer life expectancy rates, but there are also many countries that perform nearly as well with much lower spending. One reason for the discrepancy between spending and longevity is that these numbers are *average* life expectancies and *per-capita* spending rates, which mask inequalities. … Another reason … is that clean drinking water and preventive health care can be provided with little spending. If there is near universal clean water and preventive care, life expectancy rates can be high. In the U.S., however, nearly 40 million Americans lack basic health insurance, and are therefore less likely to receive preventive care. In contrast, Cuba has universal health care and one of the highest doctor-to-patient ratios in the world … It is not alone. Sri Lanka, China and the Indian State of Kerala … have adopted policies that not only reduce inequality but also increase overall health and well-being. The results of these policy priorities are significant, and can be measured in survival indicators, such as average life expectancy."

167 *Historical Tables of the White House Office of Management and Budget*, www.whitehouse.gov/omb/budget/fy2008/pdf/hist.pdf

168 See www.globalsecurity.org/military/world/spending.htm.

169 See, e.g. Henry J. Thompson, Zongjian Zhu and Weiqin Jiang, Cancer Prevention Laboratory, *Identification of the Apoptosis Activation Cascade Induced in Mammary Carcinomas by Energy Restriction*, Colorado State University, Fort Collins, Colorado, 2004.

170 See Carl Jung, *Psychological Types*, 1921. Jung described the *collective unconscious* as "archetypes," or preferences or proclivities that express themselves in art, religion, myth, and even in confronting death.

171 David Hume, *Treatise of Human Nature*, 1896.

172 See e.g. Marc D. Hauser, *Moral Minds: The Nature of Right and Wrong*, 2006

173 This is known as the Heisenberg "uncertainty principle" after Werner Heisenberg. A number of debates have arisen over whether information itself is simply the reduction of uncertainty.

174 See e.g. Eva Jablonka and Marion J. Lamb, *Evolution in Four Dimensions,* 2006.

175 Donald Kennedy in *John Gardner: A Salute, Science 22*, March 2002, explains that Gardner "had a deep grasp of the chronic paradox in American life, one noted by de Tocqueville … : Our frontier devotion to personal freedom, even license, on the one hand; and our strongly felt commitment to social order on

the other. ... [Gardner] reminds us ... that we need one another and that our society needs each of us."

176 Laura Blumenfeld, *A Time to Kill, And a Time to Heal, Washington Post,* November 25, 2007.

177 This scenario forms the basis of the novel *Logan's Run,* in which people live to 21 years old and then report to "Sleepshops" were they are drugged to death. George Clayton Johnson and William F. Nolan, *Logan's Run,* 1976.

178 See e.g. Daniel Callahan's argument in *Setting Limits,* op cite, and Gregory Stock's *Redesigning Humans: Choosing Our Genes, Changing Our Future,* 2003.

179 See David Boyd Haycock, *Mortal Coil, A Short History of Living Longer,* 2008. Haycock questions the morality of "genetically engineer[ing the patient's own cells] ... to correct a particular defect and then reintroduc[ing] them into the patient."

180 The President's Council on Bioethics, *Human Cloning and Human Dignity: An Ethical Inquiry,* July 2002, www.bioethics.gov

181 One of the first acts of President Obama, however, centered on reopening stem cell research effectively shut down by President Bush.

182 According to the National Research Council, 3% of all birth defects and developmental disabilities are caused by environmental exposures and another 25% or more may be caused by an interaction between genes and the environment. See http://www.birthdefects.org/registry/main.asp

183 A number of studies have shown that in areas with persistent food shortages and lack of medical care, the people are shorter and weigh less. See, e.g. Daniel Schwenkendiek, *Height and Weight Differences between North and South Korea, Journal of Biosocial Science,* 2009, 41:51-55: "For socioeconomic reasons, pre-school children raised in the developing country of North Korea are up to 13 cm shorter and up to 7 kg lighter than children who were brought up in South Korea ... North Korean women were also found to weight up to 9 kg less than their Southern counterparts."

184 Of course, a framework can collapse or reform or split, placing mortals in one culture and immortals in another. Jared Diamond, in *Collapse,* also makes clear that social survival isn't inevitable—the entire society could disappear.

185 *Eine neue wissenschaftliche Wahrheit pflegt sich nicht in der Weise durchzusetzen, daß ihre Gegner überzeugt werden und sich als belehrt erklären, sondern vielmehr dadurch, daß ihre Gegner allmählich aussterben und daß die heranwachsende Generation von vornherein mit der Wahrheit vertraut geworden ist.* A more literal translation is "A new scientific truth asserts itself not in the way that her opponents are persuaded and have been taught, but more often that her opponents eventually die out and the next generation grows up trusted from the start with the truth." *Wissenschaftliche Selbstbiographie.* Mit einem Bildnis und der von Max von Laue gehaltenen Traueransprache. *35 pp. (Leipzig, 1948). Scientific Autobiography and Other Papers,* trans. F. Gaynor (New York, 1949), pp.33-34 (as cited in Thomas Kuhn in *The Structure of Scientific Revolutions*).

186 My own non-scientific internet survey shows that the oldest Olympic competitors range between 61 and 72 (Oscar Swahn, from Sweden, who competed in 1920 in Antwerp) and compete in such placid things as equestrian activities or shooting. See, e.g. http://is.gd/1kAY.

187 In Russia, a governor has imposed a "sex day" to overcome the sharp decline in population after the fall of the Soviet Union—but it seems that Mother Nature already has decreed that Russia should have fewer and not more people, and the holiday has hardly enhanced the population count. The BBC reported in September 2007: *Russian "Sex Day" to Boost Births. The governor of Ulyanovsk region in Russia is offering prizes to couples who have babies in exactly nine months—on Russia's national day on 12 June.*

188 It is interesting to note, however, that the Chinese government quickly applied exemptions to the one child policy after the earthquakes in Sichuan province in the May 2008 collapse of 7000 schoolrooms, killed many children and left many others without parents. See *One-Child Policy Lifted for Quake Victims Parents, New York Times*, May 27, 2008.

189 See Simone Elegant, *Is China's One-Child Policy Heading for a Revision? Time Magazine*, July 27, 2009.

190 Richard Dawkins, *The Selfish Gene*, op cite.

191 See e.g. *Evolution in Four Dimensions*, op cite. By replicating more frequently, the chances of survival increase. By restricting replication in favor of competing relatives, the chances of reproduction of one's own genes increases.

192 Edward Lorenz, speech entitled *Predictability: Does the Flap of a Butterfly's Wings in Brazil set off a Tornado in Texas?* to the American Association for the Advancement of Science in Washington, DC, 1972

193 Op cite

194 Op cite

195 Samuel P. Huntington, *The Clash of Civilizations, Foreign Affairs*, Summer 1993. Huntington attempted to continue the Hegelian dialectic that Fukuyama tried to finish.

196 George Bernard Shaw, *The Doctor's Dilemma*, 1909. See also Kenneth Vaux, *Intending Death: Moral Perspectives*, 1977, who not only quotes Shaw, but Seneca, in his tract on suicide: "The wise man lives as long as he should, not as long as he can."

197 Catholicism wrestles over whether one should employ "ordinary" or "extraordinary" means to end or extend life. See Michael McCabe, *Ordinary Means – Extraordinary Means: A Valid Distinction?* The Nathaniel Centre, The New Zealand Catholic Bioethics Centre, 2001: "The distinction between ordinary and extraordinary means of treatment comes from a 1957 address to the International Congress of Anesthesiologists, by Pope Pius XII. This distinction has a very rich history in the Catholic manuals of moral theology. As scientific advances multiplied the medical possibilities for prolonging life, the theological and ethical questions as to what extent medical means should be employed

at the end of life became increasingly relevant. In 1951 the medicomoralist, Gerard Kelly, was among the first to define these terms: '"Ordinary means" are all medicines, treatments, and operations, which offer a reasonable hope of benefit and which can be obtained and used without excessive expense, pain, or other inconvenience. "Extraordinary means" are all medicines, treatments, and operations, which cannot be obtained or used without excessive expense, pain, or other inconvenience, or which, if used, would not offer a reasonable hope of benefit.' Pope Pius XII clarified these terms, when he said: 'But normally one is held to use only ordinary means—according to circumstances of persons, places, times, and culture—that is to say, means that do not involve any grave burden for oneself or another. A more strict obligation would be too burdensome for most people and would render the attainment of the higher, more important good too difficult.'"

198 See e.g. Merold Westphal, *God, Guilt and Death*, 1984. In his preface, discussing the benefits of the religious life, Westphal states, "[O]ver and above any benefits which might be subsumed under the heading of worldly good fortune, the crucial concern of the believing soul is to find in the sacred way of solving the problem of guilt and death. The analysis of these themes in existential terms shows their intimate linkage with each other and explains why they represent more nearly a single problem than two separate problems."

199 In a PBS program aired on New Years Day, 2008, Tom Brokaw cited the example of the exorbitant annual public cost of hospital care of a near-vegetative woman—nearly three times the income of an average family.

200 Wang Feng, Gu Baochang, Guo Zhigang, and Zhang Erli., *First systematic study of China's one-child policy reveals complexity, effectiveness of fertility regulation, Population and Development Review*, 2007. Also see http://today.uci.edu/news/release_detail.asp?key=1597

201 See e.g. Simone Elegant, *Is China's One-Child Policy Heading for a Revision? Time Magazine*, July 27, 2009. "… Xie[Lingli] noted that Shanghai will soon have to deal with a rapidly aging population. About 22% of the city's residents are over age 60—a figure that is projected to rise to 34% by 2020. The same looming problem faces China as a whole, says Wang [Feng], who points out that the number of young people entering the workforce between the ages of 20 and 24 will drop by half in the next decade. Like many other population experts outside China, Wang believes it is only a matter of time before the pressure to change the one-child policy is irresistible. 'The government should eliminate the moral barrier that's been imposed by propaganda over the past 30 years for a couple to have a second child,' says Wang. 'China should learn the lessons from other Asian countries and start acting now before it's too late.'"

202 According to a February 2, 2006 article in the Canadian *Globe and Mail*, "China is executing about 8,000 people every year, almost 20 times as many as the rest of the world combined, a new academic estimate suggests. Most of the executions are carried out with a bullet to the head, although higher-ranking people in bigger cities are sometimes executed by lethal injection. The number

of executions in China is officially a state secret. But the new estimate from academic specialists, based on information provided by local officials and judges, is likely the most accurate figure yet provided. The information was disclosed yesterday by Liu Renwen, an expert on criminal law at the Chinese Academy of Social Sciences, who said that he believes it is accurate."

203 One could cite any number of expulsions, including the Soviet movement of Chechens or the Turkish expulsions of the Armenians. The Jews may symbolize the expulsion of religionists. The Jews themselves were expelled from their original homeland in what is now Israel, then subsequently expelled from England in 1287, France in 1306, Spain in 1492, and so on throughout parts of Europe and the Middle-East until the Holocaust.

204 See, e.g. Clegg III, Claude A. *The Price of Liberty: African Americans and the Making of Liberia,* 2004; Doris Kearns Goodwin, *A Team of Rivals,* 2005. The issue that haunted both Jefferson and Lincoln was what to do with slaves once they were freed.

205 The Cherokees successfully challenged the act in the Supreme Court in *Worcester v. Georgia,* 31 U.S. (6 Pet.) 515 (1832). Chief Justice John Marshall ruled that because the Cherokee Nation was sovereign, the removal laws were invalid. The Cherokees would have to agree to removal from their own land in a Senate ratified treaty. Astoundingly, a small minority group of Cherokee signed the *Treaty of New Echota* in 1835, which the Senate and Andrew Jackson, as racist in language as any Nazi, then used as a basis to expel the Cherokee from Georgia in 1838. With little concern for food and facilities, the Cherokee were uprooted from their land, herded into what can only be described as concentration camps, and then moved in the "Trail of Tears" to North Carolina and Oklahoma.

206 "I saw the helpless Cherokees arrested and dragged from their homes, and driven at the bayonet point into the stockades. And in the chill of a drizzling rain on an October morning I saw them loaded like cattle or sheep into six hundred and forty-five wagons and started toward the west....On the morning of November the 17th we encountered a terrific sleet and snow storm with freezing temperatures and from that day until we reached the end of the fateful journey on March the 26th 1839, the sufferings of the Cherokees were awful. The trail of the exiles was a trail of death. They had to sleep in the wagons and on the ground without fire. And I have known as many as twenty-two of them to die in one night of pneumonia due to ill treatment, cold and exposure..." Private John G. Burnett, Captain Abraham McClellan's Company, 2nd Regiment, 2nd Brigade, Mounted Infantry, Cherokee Indian Removal 1838-39, quoted often, including http://www.powersource.com/cherokee/burnett.html and http://www.iwchildren.org/genocide/shame9.htm

207 Christopher R. Browning and Jurgen Matthaus, *The Origins of the Final Solution: The Evolution of Nazi Jewish Policy, September 1939-March 1942 (Comprehensive History of the Holocaust Series),* 2004.

208 *Turkey says up to 300,000 Armenians and at least as many Turks died during civil*

strife in eastern Turkey during World War I, but rejects the term "genocide." BBC article, September 1, 2005, http://news.bbc.co.uk/2/hi/europe/4205708.stm

209 See http://www.historyplace.com/worldhistory/genocide/index.html

210 See, e.g. Orlando Figes, *The Whisperers: Private Life in Stalin's Russia*, Metropolitan, 2007

211 Adopted by Resolution 260 (III) A of the United Nations General Assembly on December 9, 1948.

212 Scientists already have developed genes that light up when cancer is present. See Luke Timmerman, *Caliper Bets Future on Tools That Light Up Genes Before Researchers' Eyes*, July 28, 2008, http://www.xconomy.com/boston/2008/07/28/caliper-bets-future-on-tools-that-light-up-genes-before-researchers-eyes.

213 Eva Jablonka and Marion J. Lamb, *Evolution in Four Dimensions,* op cite